System Evaluation Theory

T0309248

A volume in
Evaluation and Society
Stewart I. Donaldson and Katrina L. Bledsoe, *Series Editors*
Jennifer Villalobos, *Managing Editor*

Evaluation and Society

Stewart I. Donaldson and Katrina L. Bledsoe, *Series Editors*
Jennifer Villalobos, *Managing Editor*

System Evaluation Theory

A Blueprint for Practitioners Evaluating Complex Interventions Operating and Functioning as Systems

Ralph Renger

Just Evaluation Services (JESS), LLC

INFORMATION AGE PUBLISHING, INC.
Charlotte, NC • www.infoagepub.com

Library of Congress Cataloging-in-Publication Data

A CIP record for this book is available from the Library of Congress
http://www.loc.gov

ISBN: 979-8-88730-042-9 (Paperback)
      979-8-88730-043-6 (Hardcover)
      979-8-88730-044-3 (E-Book)

Printed in the United States of America

Illustrations Acknowledgement

A special thank you to Macey and Mark for lending their talent
to help bring this book to life.

Contents

Prologue

> *You should only write a book when it feels urgent and like*
> *something that only you can say.*
> —Hanya Yanagihara, acclaimed novelist.[1]

Writing a book is a huge undertaking requiring sacrifices by many. My motivation and inspiration to take on this endeavor is driven by an overwhelming sense of urgency. Academics often justify their literary contributions by noting their work "fills a gap." I know, I spent over 25 years in academia. While I do feel this book fills a gap for those wanting to learn how to evaluate complex interventions operating and functioning as systems, my sense of urgency is driven by my conviction that many evaluators writing about evaluating complex interventions either have it wrong or haven't realized the full potential of evaluating such interventions as systems. My concern is that in these relatively early days of exploring the potential of systems approaches in evaluation we are creating serious damage to the field, a form of Lornez's butterfly effect: the idea that the flap of a butterfly's wing could create a sequence of events leading to a tornado. Further, "exotic" terms used by pioneering system evaluators, such as "wicked" and "super-wicked" are, in many cases, creating the unintended consequence of dissuading, rather than persuading, others from exploring the potential of

System Evaluation Theory, pages xi–xvii
Copyright © 2022 by Information Age Publishing
www.infoagepub.com
All rights of reproduction in any form reserved.

systems approaches in evaluating complex interventions. This, in turn, forms a barrier to creating the brain trust our field needs to fully explore the potential of systems approaches in evaluation. Further, the academic jargon coupled by the failure to agree on the most basic definitions, such as what defines complexity or what is meant by a system, creates the impression that we, evaluators, really don't know what we are doing. We should all be concerned about such impressions because it negatively impacts the credibility of all of us in the discipline.

I also feel as if I am one of the few who can tell the story to change this trajectory. I was blessed with a once in a lifetime opportunity and given all the necessary resources and time by the Leona M. and Harry B. Helmsley Charitable Trust to chart a way forward to explore the potential of systems approaches in evaluating complex interventions. While many evaluators, especially those in academia, are comfortable with talking the talk, I realize many evaluators interested in evaluating complex interventions haven't had the opportunities afforded me. I am fortunate to have been given the opportunity to walk the talk.

Kurt Lewin noted that there is nothing as practical as a good theory. System evaluation theory (SET) emerged from having to deal with the real-world challenges I encountered evaluating a cardiac care system of care. The cardiac care "system" is a complex intervention; consisting of many parts dependent on each other to save lives. Born out of necessity, SET bridges the theory-practice divide. Throughout this book, I illustrate the application of SET by citing examples from my own evaluations as well as drawing on universal, common experiences such as the global pandemic, family structures, and eating at restaurants. It is my hope that these real-world examples give me the credibility needed for you to listen to the way I tell the system evaluation story, a story which I hope will encourage you to pursue systems evaluation.

My Systems Evaluation Journey

This book is intended to be an important step in what my mentor Dr. Lewe Atkinson from the Haines Centre for Strategic Planning passionately refers to as a systems journey. My systems journey began in 2011 when I attended the first International Systemic Approaches in Evaluation conference hosted by the Deutsche Gesellschaft für Internationale Zusammenarbeit (GIZ) in Eschborn, Germany. It was clear that our field was struggling to understand the meaning and boundaries of systems evaluation. There wasn't even basic agreement around basic terms such as systematic, systemic, systems, and systems thinking. This meant that participants were often talking past each other.

As the conference proceeded, I began recalling the words of my friend and mentor Laura Biesedecki who often lamented that evaluators were simply selling the "flavor of the day." As I went from seminar to seminar my concern grew for the credibility of our profession. It was my summation that conference attendees saw systems evaluation as the hot new topic of discussion and even if they didn't understand it, they still felt the term had a cachet that could be marketed to make money. Not once did I hear a single colleague discuss, explain, or ask how systems evaluation could lead to social betterment.

When I raised my concerns during my seminar, I was soundly berated by my European colleagues who insisted that as academics and consultants they were the "experts." In short, they weren't worried about really understanding systems evaluation because they felt as experts they shouldn't or wouldn't be questioned. This was an upsetting experience for me and upon reflection was an inflection point in my systems evaluation journey. Leaving the conference, I was motivated to express my concerns and subsequently published an article "Systemic Evaluation, Impact Evaluation and Logic Models" with like-minded colleagues in the *Evaluation Journal of Australasia* in 2011.

Two years later I found myself in North Dakota challenged to evaluate a system with many moving parts; agencies, people, and equipment; the aforementioned cardiac system of care. All the parts needed to work in harmony and if just one part was missing or didn't work well in concert with the others, people experiencing a cardiac arrest or ST segment elevated myocardial infarction (STEMI) would die. The system was certainly complex; it had many moving and interacting parts; but I felt at its root it wasn't difficult, or complicated, to understand.

I set out looking for a path forward, that is, for an evaluation theory, to help guide me in how to evaluate this complex intervention. I began by seeking out sessions at international conferences. There were many sessions devoted to the topic of evaluating complexity. I came to learn that one promising avenue to evaluating complexity was systems thinking. But as I read more, I had a flashback to the GIZ 2011 conference and I realized that the discussion of systems thinking was centered on solving the limitations of applying program evaluation methods to address complexity. This was a second inflection point in my systems evaluation journey and where this book begins. As you will learn in Chapter 1, evaluators have long recognized that tools, like the logic model, were not suited to handle complexity. Thus, I was surprised to learn that many evaluators were advocating for using *more* logic models, aka coupling and scaffolding, to evaluate complex interventions. As Einstein was purported to have said, "You can't solve problems with the thinking that gave rise to them." It made no sense to me that the solution to evaluating complex interventions was to apply more of something that was already deemed inadequate.

It was my assessment that our field was trying to solve the game of chess (i.e., evaluating complexity) by playing checkers (i.e., linear thinking). We needed to move from what Chris Argyris called single loop learning to double and triple loop learning. Single loop learning is continually trying the things you are familiar with and know how to do in the hope it will work. The colloquial definition of insanity is to keep trying the same thing and expecting a different result. So, I engaged in double loop and triple loop learning, searching for a better path forward by first revisiting the basic assumptions of complexity. What I learned is that complexity was not novel at all and has been the focus of theorists studying systems for decades. Further, these theorists had made significant strides in defining system properties that had the potential to pave a new path forward for evaluators to meaningfully begin to evaluate complex interventions. I just needed to align the evaluation approach to these system properties in such a way that made it accessible and applicable for evaluation practitioners.

I approached The Leona M. and Harry B. Helmsley Charitable Trust and shared with them that if they wanted the cardiac care system evaluated, then we would have to develop the approach to do so. They agreed and provided me the time and resources to develop a theory to guide the evaluation of complex interventions acting as systems. I am forever indebted to the Trust for that opportunity, an opportunity that was the third inflection point on my systems evaluation journey.

I began by hiring a biologist to help me understand what makes a system a system. Through these interactions I began to more fully appreciate the relationship between the system properties of interdependence and emergence. It is these two fundamental properties that form the foundation for SET. As I continued my work with the biologist, I soon learned I was encumbered by my reductionist training as an experimental psychologist. Reductionists are trained to break everything into small parts. For them, as Russel Ackoff explained, everything can be explained by a linear, cause and effect relationship. Reductionist thinking is antithetical to systems thinking, which emphasizes synthesis, that is how things work together, often nonlinearly, to achieve an emerging purpose. The holistic perspective has significant implications on how we think about evaluating the success of complex interventions acting as systems.

I also came to realize, as I detail in the book's last chapter, that the thinking of colleagues who were similarly educated as me, but did not make the transition in thinking from reductionism to synthesis, acted as an impediment to evaluation generally, but especially to systems evaluation. In his 2013 address at the AES annual conference in Brisbane, Michael Scriven aptly warned that reductionist researchers have hijacked our field and view evaluators as "intellectual outcasts." Indeed, I experienced this firsthand, during what can only be described as an all-out personal attack during a talk I gave at the 2014 CES annual conference in Ottawa. Many researchers, operating under the guise of evaluators, are steadfast in their belief that the randomized control trial (RCT) is the gold standard of evaluation methodology. When I challenged them, I was summarily dismissed and belittled. It was clear these "evaluators" either did not understand or refused to accept that, as Levin-Rozalis eloquently summarized in her 2003 publication in the *Canadian Journal of Program Evaluation*, research and evaluation are not the same thing. Research is traditionally about knowledge development, evaluation about providing information to inform decision-making. We need to ensure we question and think critically about the application of research methods to evaluation problems because they may be inappropriate, irresponsible, and in some cases unethical. As you will learn, it is my position that both reductionist and holistic thinking are needed to complete an evaluation of a complex intervention. One way of thinking is not superior to the other nor should supplant the other; they are complimentary.

SET is intended to act as a blueprint for evaluators, guiding them through how to evaluate a complex intervention operating and functioning as a system. In developing and validating SET, Kurt Lewin's words on the practicality of a good theory acted as my North Star. Yet, despite my numerous practice-based examples, some reviewers were critical of my work, noting a heavy United States-based bias. I am unapologetic. Everything has its start somewhere, and SET emerged from the work in evaluating the cardiac care system in seven rural states in the United States of America. Nevertheless, as you will learn, since it was first published in 2015, SET has been applied to evaluate complex interventions operating in many sectors throughout the world.

Some reviewers of the book also criticized how I present SET, pointing out that the SET's three steps are very linear which is in direct opposition to system thinking. My rebuttal is that the way a method is taught should not be conflated with the product of that method. You can't show someone a puzzle and expect them to understand how the pieces went together to form an impression. You need to first show how the pieces fit together. My building block approach to teaching is indeed linear, but what emerges from those building blocks is a comprehensive approach to defining and evaluating complex interventions acting as systems.

By this point in the prologue, I hope you have discerned that my intent is to write with candor. Throughout the book I endeavor to be self-critical, pointing out my mistakes in my systems journey and how I would do things differently, or better, given another chance. I am also critical of many systems thinking pioneers in evaluation, and I have been criticized for being critical of them. However, my criticisms should not be mistaken for disrespect. It was the thoughts of Meadows, Cabrera, Trochim, Checkland, Ison, and Rogers that inspired deep personal reflection from which SET emerged. I cannot think of a higher form of praise than someone's work inspiring others. I fully expect there will be those who will be critical of SET, and I welcome their criticism. I will respect that criticism if it is followed by a better path forward so that our field can make the advancements needed to provide stakeholders with the most meaningful and useful information to assist decision-making.

My systems evaluation journey would not have been possible without the support of critical friends, mentors, and family. I am grateful to Dr. Michelle Irving, Mr. Brian Keogh, and Dr. Carlos Rodriguez for their honesty in questioning the "Why?" behind every, and I mean every, aspect of my thinking. To my friend Mark Pearce and his daughter Macey, whose creativity and illustrations helped bring clarity and life to my thoughts, thank you.

I am also deeply indebted to my two mentors Drs. Melanie Pescud and Lewe Atkinson. Mel, I can never repay you for the time you invested in helping make this book a reality. You are the deepest, most reflective thinker I have encountered in my career, and you have the most thoughtful way of redirecting negativity into positivity. Lewe, thank you for being my system's journey guide.

Finally, I am nothing without my family. To my daughter Jessica I want to say "thank you Munch" for never complaining when intended relaxing dad-daughter walks turned into mini systems think tanks. To my daughter Jenna, I want to say "thank you Boo" for keeping me grounded in reality. You taught me that although the world is complex, it doesn't have to be complicated: ice cream makes it all okay. And finally, to my wife, Kitka, thank you for your continued encouragement and belief in me.

Note

1. NPR interview with Scott Simon, January 8, 2022. https://www.npr.org/ 2022/01/08/1071542929/hanya-yanagiharas-to-paradise-is-one-of-the -most-highly-anticipated-novels-of-20

1

The Rise of Systems Thinking
in Evaluation

*We cannot solve the problems associated with evaluating complexity with the
same level of thinking that gave rise to them.*

—Albert Einstein, translated

We can't play chess using checkers thinking.

Most of the intellectual capital in our [evaluation] discipline is invested in evaluating programs. The thousands of presentations at
professional conferences and publications in evaluation journals worldwide devoted to improving the science of program evaluation attest
to the dominant focus of the program as the object of the evaluation,
that is, the evaluand (Scriven, 1991). The focus of this book, however,
is on an evaluand receiving relatively little attention in the evaluation
literature despite being considered a top two priority area in our discipline's future: complex interventions operating and functioning as
systems (Patton, 2013).

System Evaluation Theory, pages 1–19
Copyright © 2022 by Information Age Publishing
www.infoagepub.com
1

The term *system* is used throughout the book to refer to complex interventions operating and functioning as a system. Further, the term intervention is all-encompassing including, but not limited to activities, projects, programs, policies, and complex interventions acting as systems. Interventions vary in their level of complexity. As you will learn in this chapter, the term complexity means different things to different evaluators. In this chapter, I define complexity and differentiate it from complicated. I also discuss the root causes for the challenges evaluators are having in evaluating complexity. In Chapters 2–4, I provide evaluators the knowledge and guidance necessary to differentiate whether the complex intervention is intentionally organized to operate and function as a system or is just a "bunch of stuff" (Meadows, 2008).

Before delving into the why and how of evaluating complex interventions acting as systems it is time well spent to understand the genesis of this book's focus: System evaluation theory (SET; Figure 1.1; Renger, 2015). As Dr. Carl Sagan (1980) said "You have to know the past to understand the present." Many evaluation theories and methods evolve as part

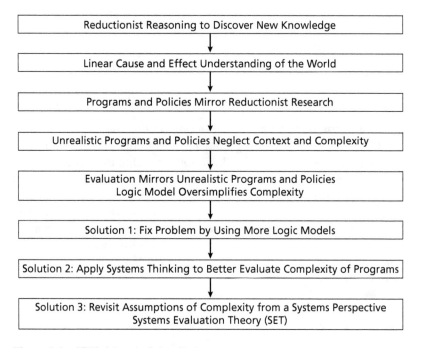

Figure 1.1   SET's historical timeline.

of an iterative problem-solving process: As evaluators encounter a problem, they develop a solution. That solution in turn creates an obstacle that requires another solution. SET evolved in the same way; it is part of a long problem-solving thread. To understand this evolution is to understand the *why* behind SET. This understanding will help orient your decision-making; it will help you determine whether SET is the appropriate approach for the challenge you are faced with evaluating (Sweet, 2017). I do not consider SET an endpoint in the problem-solving process. As others read my work and understand how SET came to be, it is my hope they will continue to evolve SET or develop new and better approaches for evaluating complex interventions acting as systems. The story of SET begins by understanding the premise of the reductionist research paradigm and how this influences intervention design and evaluation.

The Reductionist Paradigm

The purpose of research is to discover new knowledge (Levin-Rozalis, 2003; Mark et al., 2000). Once research has been reliably replicated and validated the focus then switches to applying that new knowledge for social betterment (Levin-Rozalis, 2003; Mark et al., 2000; Suchman 1967). Mechanisms for applying new knowledge, that is to bridge research into practice, include policies, programs, and complex interventions (Green & Kreuter, 2005).

In the 1960s there was a reckoning that the designs and methods used in our pursuit of knowledge were not useful when attempting to *apply* that knowledge (Mark et al., 2000; Suchman, 1967). The problem was that the research was based on "the traditional pattern of thinking... built on the hypothesis of atomism with characteristics of linearity and causal determinism, so it cannot be applied to the complex and non-linear stochastic problem" (Wulun, 2007, p. 395).

Wulun's (2007) explanation of the problems associated with trying to apply research grounded in reductionism to the real world can be challenging to understand because of his heavy use of "academic speak" (Federation University, 2021). I was an academic for almost 30 years and I always felt many of my colleagues were creating unnecessary barriers by using academic speak. One of my earliest and now late mentors, Dr. Barb Brown, a sociologist, referred to the use of academic speak as a type of conspicuous-consumption: Basically, you feel like you need to act the part so people believe how you are presenting yourself. I feel quite the opposite. I believe an expert should ideally be able to explain whatever it is she/he does to an 8-year-old in a 20-second elevator ride (Renger et al., 2007). With that perspective, I will endeavor to explain the challenges faced in applying reductionist research to the real world by using a jigsaw puzzle analogy.

Imagine social problems as giant jigsaw puzzles to be solved. Figure 1.2 shows an example of what a jigsaw puzzle might look like for the problem of obesity. There are a few things that Figure 1.2 helps to illustrate. First, you will notice the puzzle shape is asymmetrical. This reflects the reality that each social problem is unique and doesn't fit into a neat, tidy box. Second, the puzzle is complex; it has many multi-sided and interlocking pieces. Third, the puzzle boundary is intentionally depicted without the traditional straight edges. This serves as a reminder that we

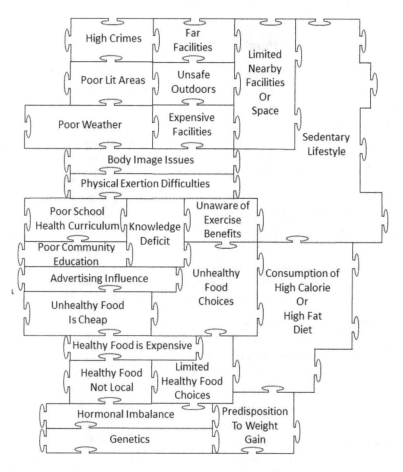

Figure 1.2 The obesity jigsaw puzzle.

may not have the complete picture. Fourth, all the puzzle pieces are needed to complete the picture (i.e., an understanding) of obesity; no single puzzle piece provides the complete picture of obesity. In systems language, the connecting puzzle pieces are termed interdependent. The picture they create together is called emergence. You will learn more about the system properties of interdependence and emergence in the next chapter and their implications on evaluating complex interventions acting as systems in Chapters 8 and 9, respectively.

> The terms *complex* and *complicated* are used differently and inter-changeably by different evaluators (and indeed within the field of re-search) when it comes to systems. For example, Rogers (2008) uses the term complicated to describe a system that has many moving parts and the term complex to describe what emerges as a result of these interactions. Williams and van't Hof (2016), define a complex system as having more moving parts, and complicated to describe the sophistication in which the parts are interrelated. Merriam-Webster (n.d.) dictionary defines both complex and complicated as consisting of many intractably combined parts. Throughout this book the term complex is used to convey the idea of many moving parts within a intervention, while complicated is used to express the sentiment of something being difficult.

Researchers operating from the reductionist paradigm try to solve the obesity puzzle by taking the puzzle apart; breaking it down into a series of linear relationships between a few individual puzzle pieces. For example, there is abundant research focused on the dietary aspects of obesity. This body of research has drilled down to show that consuming a high calorie diet is a contributor to obesity. If calories consumed is greater than calories burned, then weight gain and obesity ensue (Howell & Kones, 2017; Kämpfen & Mauer, 2016). In trying to explain why this calorie imbalance occurs researchers drilled down further and learned that some people choose to eat high-calorie foods because it is their perception that they are cheaper than healthy choice alternatives. The puzzle pieces related to this line of research are shown in Figure 1.3. I refer to the set of puzzle pieces embodying this singular line of research as a thread.

There is yet another body of research that is focused on understanding how physical activity, a mitigating factor for obesity, is influenced by the physical environment. This research discovered that the farther away the gym, or park, or bike path is from a person's home the

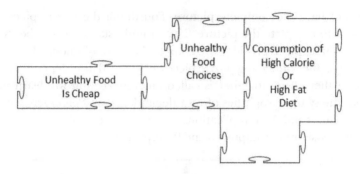

Figure 1.3 Some of the nutritional-based root causes of obesity.

less likely they are to get out and be physically active (Reed & Phillips, 2010). This puzzle thread is shown in Figure 1.4.

Still other obesity research has focused on the predisposition to weight gain, drilling down to genetic factors (Farooqi & O'Rahilly, 2006). This puzzle thread is shown in Figure 1.5.

There are of course many other research studies devoted to study-ing different obesity puzzle pieces and threads. However, regardless of

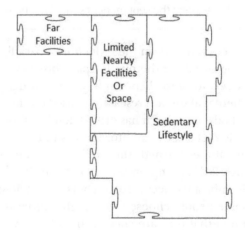

Figure 1.4 Some of the environmental root causes of obesity.

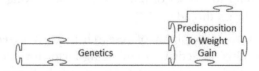

Figure 1.5 Genetic predisposition of obesity.

the puzzle pieces being studied, the reductionist paradigm is focused on trying to establish cause and effect relationships for a few puzzle pieces at a time.

Applying Reductionist Research: Implications on Intervention Design

As noted above, the purpose of discovering new knowledge is to apply that knowledge to improve society in some way. For interventions to be effective they must be designed to work in concert with the world in which they are intended to operate; they must be holistically designed. By definition this means they will have many moving parts, they will be complex. Unfortunately, too often, interventions do not mirror the reality of the problem. Instead, their design is grounded in reductionist research, designed to focus on a single puzzle thread. For example, educational programs are used to change perceptions of the cost of healthy food, policies are implemented to improve the physical environment to encourage physical activity, and there are genetic interventions for obesity.

When interventions mirror the reductionist research, that is, when they are designed to focus on a small, linear part of the puzzle, they have little chance of demonstrating impact. In my opinion, the evidence of this design flaw lies in the evaluation findings that show the majority of programs fail (GAO, 2004, Suchman, 1967). To illustrate why interventions designed this way fail, my colleagues and I suggested using what we called a context map (Renger et al., 2015). The context map depicts numerous underlying conditions of obesity validated by research grounded in the reductionist paradigm. The boxes highlighted in gray in Figure 1.6 are those being targeted by a hypothetical intervention. By placing the intervention in context, it becomes immediately evident that there are many underlying conditions over which the intervention has no direct and immediate influence to change (Huntington & Renger, 2003; Renger et al., 2015). In fact, as you move from left (immediate outcomes) to right (intermediate and long-term outcomes) in the context map, the likelihood the intervention can demonstrate change becomes smaller and smaller. The visual in Figure 1.6 has proven time and again to be very useful in helping manage funders' expectations regarding the outcomes for which interventions should be held accountable and for the need to design complex interventions that are coordinated to address multiple underlying conditions.

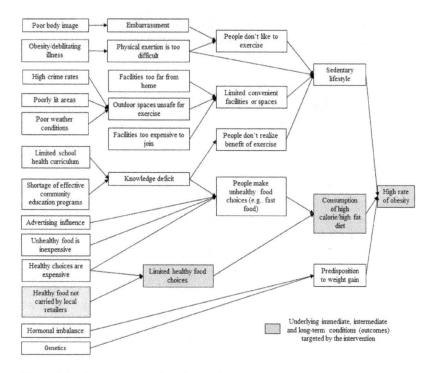

Figure 1.6 A context map for obesity.

When evaluating interventions designed to target single puzzle threads of a complex puzzle, the evaluation approach is moot. No evaluation method can compensate for a poor intervention design.

In working with clients, who are committed to interventions focused on single puzzle threads I hold them accountable for changes to immediate outcomes. I do insist that their interventions show their relationship to the broader context (i.e., the long-term outcome), but suggest that they do not commit to showing change in long-term outcomes over which they have little direct control to change.

A Visual Way to Summarizing the Challenges of the Reductionist Paradigm in Evaluation

The old adage is that a picture is worth 1,000 words. I believe the photos shown in Figure 1.7 sum up nicely the perspective of reductionist research and why this perspective does not translate well when designing and evaluating interventions. An intervention must be designed with a bigger picture perspective and the evaluation approach aligned to this perspective.

The Challenge of Evaluating Well-Designed, Complex Interventions

When interventions *are* designed to address the complexity of the underlying conditions giving rise to the problem they are trying to solve, evaluators have struggled trying to evaluate them. In my experience, the primary reason evaluators struggle is that they are trying to use methods with which they are familiar, rather than those fit for purpose. The most obvious example of this is in trying to use the logic model to evaluate complex interventions.

(a)   (b)

Figure 1.7 (a) Reductionist perspective and the program logic model. (b) Systems perspective and system evaluation theory (SET).

The purpose of a well-constructed logic model is to summarize the "logical" relationships between the program theory, the intervention, and the expected outcomes (Chen, 1990; Donaldson, 2005, Hawkins, 2020; Renger & Titcomb, 2002; Weiss, 1995). The puzzle thread being targeted by an intervention is referred to as a program theory (Chen, 1990; Donaldson, 2005; Weiss, 1995). Using a logic model to summarize only the key intervention elements was done out of the desire to achieve clarity through simplicity (Hummelbrunner, 2011). Table 1.1 is an example of a logic model summary table for the diet and obesity puzzle thread depicted in Figure 1.6.

Rogers (2008, 2010) has suggested using multiple logic models to evaluate complex interventions by essentially creating a logic model for each component (i.e., puzzle thread) of the intervention. This has been referred to as coupling or scaffolding logic models (Cabrera & Trochim, 2006; Walton et al., 2021). The problem with this approach is that each logic model is "linearly myopic." This is an artifact caused by program theory mirroring the if–then thinking underpinning the reductionist, cause-and-effect research (Ackoff, 1971, 1994; McLaughlin & Jordan, 1999; Renger & Titcomb, 2002). Thus, when using logic models, we may never open our eyes to consider the need to evaluate the important, nonlinear connections between the intervention components necessary for its success.

To help remind emerging evaluators of the limitations of the logic model for evaluating intervention complexity, I suggest they depict the logic model outcomes as puzzle pieces instead of columns, like that shown in Table 1.2. Such a depiction serves to reinforce the idea that there are important connections not addressed by the intervention and thus not considered in the evaluation.

Certainly, there are some instances where the underlying conditions of a problem being targeted for intervention are straightforward and linearly related. In these situations, using a logic model will not distort the reality (Renger et al., 2020). There is no sense in unnecessarily complicating matters. As Williams (2010) noted "the key [evaluation approach] must fit the lock [the evaluand]." However, common sense tells us that the world is complex and the relationships are rarely, if ever, linear.

TABLE 1.1   A Logic Model for the Diet and Obesity Puzzle Thread

Program Assumptions	Intervention	Inputs	Outputs	Outcomes		
				Immediate	Intermediate	Long Term
If we change people's perceptions about unhealthy food being cheap, then they will make healthier food choices, this in turn will lead to a consumption of lower calorie diets, which will decrease the incidence of obesity.	A series of educational workshops	• Instructor costs • Marketing costs • Rental space	• Number of workshop sessions • Number of participants • Workshop manuals • Trained instructors	Change in perceptions	Better food choices	• Balanced caloric intake • Reduction in obesity

TABLE 1.2 An Alternative Program Logic Model to Remind Us of the Reality in Which Outcomes Are Related

Intervention	Inputs	Outputs	Outcomes
A series of educational workshops	• Instructor costs • Marketing costs • Rental space	• Number of workshop sessions • Number of participants • Trained instructors	

In my early work with logic models, I defended the linear presentation of program assumptions (Renger & Hurley, 2006). I argued then that one benefit of reductionist methods like root cause analysis (and its resulting linear depiction of underlying conditions) was that it made it clearer where to intervene; namely, at the start of the causal sequence. I have come to realize that this position is oversimplistic and can lead to findings that don't align with intuition, undermine trust, and jeopardize the use of evaluation findings. In my defense my systems skills were still germinating!

Consequences of Using the Program Logic Model to Evaluate Complex Interventions on Evaluation Utility

When we use logic models to evaluate complex interventions it may undermine, to borrow a research term, the face validity of the evaluation. Mencken once wrote "for every complex problem there is an answer that is clear, simple, and wrong" (Brainy Quote, 2021). Research tells us that decision-makers are suspicious of simple solutions that do not align with their understanding of the complexity of their interventions (Barlow & Stone, 2011; Byrne, 2019). As such, they may not trust the evaluation findings based on the logic model and may ignore them in their decision-making calculus (Patton, 2008). This is highly problematic because evaluation utility is one of the program evaluation standard pillars (Yarbourogh et al., 2010) and many argue a gold standard by which the success of an evaluation is judged. If the purpose of an evaluation is to inform decision-making, but the evaluation findings are not being used to inform decisions, then clearly the evaluation was a failure.

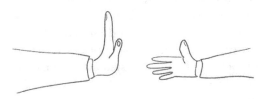

Russel Ackoff (1994) famously said: "If we didn't meet or exceed expectations of the client, then it's [the evaluation] a failure, no matter what academics think."

Toward a Better Solution: Systems Thinking

The concerns of evaluating complex interventions using methods not fit for purpose have been articulated by evaluators for some time (Hawkins, 2020; Patton, 2013; Rogers, 2000; Richmond & Peterson, 2001; Stufflebeam, 2004), although it took almost a decade for solutions to these problems to emerge. One such solution is systems thinking.

There are numerous and often confusing definitions of systems thinking (GIZ, 2011; Monat & Gannon, 2015). Davis and Stroink (2016) define systems thinking as "a trans-disciplinary construct that has been promoted as a means of being able to better comprehend and mitigate complex social-ecological dilemmas" (p. 576). For this book's purpose we need a common understanding of what we mean by systems thinking. The simplest definition is that systems thinking is literally a way of thinking about systems (Ossimitz, 1996). I find the definition by Arnold and Wade (2015) better aligned with the practitioner-based approach of this book:

> Systems thinking is a set of synergistic analytic skills used to improve the capability of identifying and understanding systems, predicting their behaviors, and devising modifications to them in order to produce desired effects. These skills work together as a system. (p. 7)

The rationale for exploring the potential of systems thinking to assist in evaluating complex interventions is straightforward: Since systems are complex, then adopting this way of thinking should help in evaluating complex interventions operating and functioning as systems.

The three system thinking notions receiving the most attention in the evaluation literature are boundaries, interrelationships, and perspectives (Williams & van 't Hof, 2016). The work of Williams and his colleagues is heavily based on that by Cabrera (for which Cabrera does not get the deserved credit) and so dominates the systems thinking evaluation landscape that you should not be surprised to encounter colleagues who believe these three systems notions, pardon the pun, encompass the entire "boundaries" of systems thinking. As a valued colleague of mine, Michelle Irving once quipped, "It's as though these three systems ideas have been 'hi-jacked' and evaluators have no awareness of the breadth of system principles" (personal communication, January 15, 2021). As you will learn throughout this book there are many other system principles that can benefit evaluators in evaluating complex interventions acting as systems.

One important thing to understand as it relates to how systems thinking evolved in evaluation is that Williams and his colleagues advocate for the use of systems thinking to *address the limitations in evaluating the* program *evaluand* (Williams & Hummelbrunner, 2010; Williams & van 't Hof, 2016). Systems thinking was the "fix" for limitations with program evaluation methods like the logic model. As a son of a carpenter, I learned the importance of setting a proper foundation (i.e., design) and that there are a cascading set of problems caused by a poor foundation that you just can't fix no matter what tools are in your toolbox. It is this philosophy that motivated me to develop a blueprint for evaluating complex interventions operating and functioning as systems: System evaluation theory (SET).

In the next chapter you will learn how to recognize whether a systems approach is the best fit for evaluating the intervention you are challenged to evaluate. Assuming a systems approach is the right one, you will learn how to methodically define all the intervention puzzle pieces and how they interlock. With this foundation in place, you will then learn how to evaluate the relationships within and between intervention components. Finally, you will learn how to evaluate the entire picture, that is when all the intervention components work together as they should.

Conclusion

In this chapter I explained how the reductionist paradigm influences intervention design and the methods to evaluate them. The problem is that many interventions are not designed to mirror the complex reality of the social problem they are intended to remedy; often only focusing on a small component of the social problem. Thus, it should come as no surprise to anyone why so many fall short in changing the outcomes they were designed to change (GAO, 2004; Suchman, 1967).

When interventions *are* designed with the necessary complexity, evaluators struggle with how to evaluate them, trying to use methods like the logic model they are familiar with rather than approaches fit for that purpose. Some evaluators suggest using additional logic models to better capture an intervention's complexity. Doing more of what you know to solve a novel problem is called single loop thinking (Argyris, 1976). If we want our evaluations to better capture the complexity of the interventions, then we need to engage in double-loop and triple loop learning (Argyris, 1976). That is, we must begin by establishing the underlying assumptions of complexity and then tailor an approach that is based on those assumptions.

It was how evaluators were trying to deal with evaluating complexity in a program evaluation context by applying systems thinking that stimulated my thinking and served as a bridge to SET. SET is by no means an endpoint to the problem-solving process and, as such, I encourage other evaluators to continue to evolve the way the field thinks about evaluating systems.

In the next chapter you will learn that complexity and systems are inextricably linked. You will be introduced to two key system properties, interdependence and emergence that provide the key to unlocking the evaluation of complex interventions. In Chapter 5 you will learn how SET is deliberately aligned to evaluate these properties, thus completing the story of why SET evolved as it did.

References

Ackoff, R. (1971). Towards a system of systems concepts. *Management Science, 17*(11), 661–671. https://doi.org/10.1287/mnsc.17.11.661

Ackoff, R. (1994). *If Russ Ackoff had given a TED talk* [Video]. https://www.youtube.com/watch?v=OqEeIG8aPPk

Argyris, C. (1976). Single-loop and double-loop models in research on decision-making. *Administrative Science Quarterly, 21*(3), 363–375. https://doi.org/10.2307/2391848

Arnold, R. D., & Wade, J. P. (2015). A definition of systems thinking: A systems approach. *Procedia Computer Science, 44*, 669–678. https://doi.org/10.1016/j.procs.2015.03.050

Barlow, Z., & Stone, M. K. (2011). Living systems and leadership: Cultivating conditions for institutional change. *Journal of Sustainability Education, 2*(1), 1–29.

Brainy Quote. (2021). *H. L. Mencken quotes.* https://www.brainyquote.com/quotes/h_l_mencken_129796

Byrne, B. (2019). *Simple solution and complex problems—A lethal combination.* https://kinchlyons.com/simple-solutions-and-complex-problems-a-lethal-combination/

Cabrera, D., & Trochim, W. M. K. (2006). A theory of systems evaluation. In D. Cabrera (Ed.), *Systems evaluation and evaluation systems whitepaper series.* Cornell University.

Chen, H. T. (1990). *Theory-driven evaluation.* SAGE Publications.

Davis, A. C., & Stroink, M. L. (2016). The relationship between systems thinking and the new ecological paradigm. *Systems Research and Behavioral Science, 33*(4), 575–586. https://doi.org/10.1002/sres.2371

Donaldson, S. I. (2005). Using program theory-driven evaluation science to crack the Da Vinci code. *New Directions for Evaluation, 2005*(106), 65–84. https://doi.org/10.1002/ev.152

Farooqi, I. S., & O'Rahilly, S. O. (2006). Genetics of obesity in humans. *Endocrine Reviews, 27*(7), 710–718. https://doi.org/10.1210/er.2006-0040

Federation University. (2021). *University speak: Linking words and phrases.* https://studyskills.federation.edu.au/wp-content/uploads/2020/06/university-speak_2020.pdf

GAO. (2004). *OMB's program assessment rating tool presents opportunities and challenges for budget and performance integration.* https://www.gao.gov/assets/gao-04-439t.pdf

GIZ. (2011, January). *Conference proceedings.* Deutsche Gesellschaft fur International Zusammenarbeit (GIZ) Systemic Evaluation Conference, Eschborn, Germany.

Green, L. W., & Kreuter, M. W. (2005). *Health promotion planning: An educational and ecological approach* (3rd ed.). Mayfield Publishing Company. https://doi.org/10.1007/BF03404986

Hawkins, A. (2020). Program logic foundations: Putting the logic back into program logic. *Journal of MultiDisciplinary Evaluation, 16*(37), 38–57. https://journals.sfu.ca/jmde/index.php/jmde_1/article/view/657

Howell, S., & Kones, R. (2017). "Calories in, calories out" and macronutrient intake: The hope, hype, and science of calories. *American Journal of Physiology: Endocrinology and Metabolism, 313*(5), E608–E612. https://doi.org/10.1152/ajpendo.00156.2017

Hummelbrunner, R. (2011). Systems thinking and evaluation. *Evaluation, 17*(4), 395–403. https://doi.org/10.1177/1356389011421935

Huntington, C., & Renger, R. (2003). *Response to the OMB performance and management assessment of the health professions program.* Testimony submitted to the Interdisciplinary Committee on Community Based Linkages reporting to HRSA.

Kämpfen, F., & Maurer, J. (2016). Time to burn (calories)? The impact of retirement on physical activity among mature Americans. *Journal of Health Economics, 45*, 91–102. https://doi.org/10.1016/j.jhealeco.2015.12.001

Levin-Rozalis, M. (2003). Evaluation and research: Differences and similarities. *Canadian Journal of Program Evaluation, 18*(2), 1–31.

Mark, M. M., Henry, G. T., & Julnes, G. (2000). *Evaluation: An integrated framework for understanding, guiding, and improving policies and programs.* Jossey-Bass.

McLaughlin, J. A., & Jordan, G. B. (1999). Logic models: A tool for telling your program's performance story. *Evaluation and Program Planning, 22*(1), 65–72. https://doi.org/10.1016/S0149-7189(98)00042-1

Meadows, D. (2008). *Thinking in systems: A primer.* Chelsea Green Publishing.

Merriam-Webster. (n.d.). Complex. In *Merriam-Webster.com dictionary.* Retrieved January 1, 2022, from https://www.merriam-webster.com/dictionary/complex

Monat, J. P., & Gannon, T. F. (2015). What is systems thinking? A review of selected literature plus recommendations. *American Journal of Systems Science, 4*(1), 11–26.

Ossimitz, G. (1996). *The development of systems thinking skills using systems dynamics modelling tools.* http://webdoc.sub.gwdg.de/ebook/e/gdm/1996/ossimitz.pdf

Patton, M. Q. (2008). *Utilization-focused evaluation.* SAGE Publications. https://doi.org/10.1177/1098214010373646

Patton, M. (2013). The future of evaluation in society: Top ten trends plus one. In S. I. Donaldson (Ed.), *The future of evaluation and society: A tribute to Michael Scriven* (pp. 45–62). Information Age Publishing.

Reed, J. A., & Phillips, D. E. (2010). Relationships between physical activity and the proximity of exercise facilities and home exercise equipment used by undergraduate university students. *Journal of American College Health, 53*(6), 285–290. https://doi.org/10.3200/JACH.53.6.285-290

Renger, R. (2015). System evaluation theory (SET). *Evaluation Journal of Australasia, 15*(4), 16–28. https://doi.org/10.1177/1035719X1501500403

Renger, R., & Hurley, C. (2006). From theory to practice: Lessons learned in the application of the ATM approach to developing logic models. *Evaluation and Program Planning, 29*(2), 106–119. https://doi.org/10.1016/j.evalprogplan.2006.01.004

Renger, R., & Titcomb, A. (2002). A three-step approach to teaching logic models. *American Journal of Evaluation, 23*(4), 493–503. https://doi.org/10.1177/109821400202300409

Renger, R., Foltysova, J., Becker, K., & Souvannasacd, E. (2015). The power of the context map: Designing realistic outcome evaluation strategies and other unanticipated benefits. *Evaluation and Program Planning, 52*, 118–125. https://doi.org/10.1016/j.evalprogplan.2015.04.003

Renger, R., Page, M., & Renger, J. (2007). What an eight-year-old can teach us about logic modelling and mainstreaming. *The Canadian Journal of Program Evaluation, 22*(1), 195–204.

Renger, R., Foltysova, J., Renger, J., Donaldson, S. I., Hart, G., & Hawkins, A. (2020). Comparing and contrasting a program versus system approach to evaluation: The example of a cardiac care system. *Canadian Journal of Program Evaluation, 35*(2), 240–257. https://doi.org/10.3138/cjpe.68127

Richmond, B., & Peterson, S. (2001). *An introduction to systems thinking.* High Performance Systems.

Rogers, P. J. (2008). Using programme theory to evaluate complicated and complex aspects of interventions. *Evaluation, 14*(1), 29–48. https://doi.org/10.1177/1356389007084674

Rogers, P. J. (2000) 'Causal models in program theory evaluation. In P. J. Rogers, A. J. Petrosino, T. Hacsi, & T. A. Huebner (Eds.), *Program theory evaluation: Challenges and opportunities* (pp. 47–55). Jossey-Bass.

Rogers, P. J. (2010, November 10–13). *Representing simple, complicated, and complex aspects in logic models for evaluation quality.* The 24th Annual Conference of the American Evaluation Association, San Antonio, Texas.

Sagan, C. E. (Writer), Druyan, A. (Writer), & Soter, S. (Writer), & Malone A. (Director). (1980, October 5). One voice in the cosmic fugue (Episode 2) [Television series episode]. In G. Andorfer & R. McCain (Producers), *Cosmos: A Personal Voyage.* Public Broadcasting Service.

Scriven, M. (1991). *Evaluation thesaurus* (4th ed.). SAGE Publications.

Stufflebeam, D. L. (2004). The 21st Century CIPP Model. In M. C. Alkin (Ed.), *Evaluation Roots* (pp. 245–66). SAGE Publications. https://dx.doi.org/10.4135/9781412984157.n16

Suchman, E. A. (1967). *Evaluative research: Principles and practice in public service and social action programs.* Russel Sage Foundation.

Sweet, P. (2017). *The importance of knowing your "why."* https://engineering-managementinstitute.org/knowing-your-why/

Walton, M., Gates, E. F., & Vidueira, P. (2021). Insights and future directions for systems and complexity-informed evaluation. *New Directions for Evaluation, 170,* 159–171. https://doi.org/10.1002/ev.20459

Weiss, C. H. (1995). Nothing as practical as a good theory: Exploring theory-based evaluation for comprehensive community initiatives for children and families. In J. P. Connell, A. C. Kubisch, L. B. Schorr, & C. H. Weiss (Eds.), *New Approaches to Evaluating Community Initiatives* (pp. 65–69). Aspen Institute.

Williams, B. (2010, November 8–13). *Fitting the key to the lock: Matching systems methods to evaluation questions.* The 24th annual conference of the American Evaluation Association, San Antonio, Texas, United States.

Williams, B., & Hummelbrunner, R. (2010). *Systems concepts in action: A practitioner's toolkit.* Stanford University Press.

Williams, B. & van 't Hof, S. (2016). *Wicked solutions: A systems approach to wicked problems* (2nd ed.). Bob Williams.

Wulun, J. (2007). Understanding complexity, challenging traditional ways of thinking. *Systems Research and Behavioral Science, 24,* 393–402. https://doi.org/10.1002/sres.840

Yarbrough, D. B., Shula, L. M., Hopson, R. K., & Caruthers, F. A. (2010). *The program evaluation standards: A guide for evaluators and evaluation users* (3rd ed). Corwin Press.

2

What Is a System?

You need to understand what you are evaluating before you can evaluate it.

In Chapter 1, you learned that evaluators have explored different ways to address the limitations of program evaluation approaches (e.g., the logic model), in evaluating complex interventions. I believe that authors like Cabrera and Checkland were on the right track in suggesting that systems thinking might be the solution to better evaluating complexity. However, in reading more about complexity, I came to the realization that complexity is inextricably intertwined with an understanding of systems (Holland, 1992). Therefore, it was my conclusion that many evaluators trying to evaluate complexity struggled because they viewed complexity as a "bunch of stuff" (Meadows, 2008). A bunch of stuff does not provide any standards to which an evaluation could be anchored. To move evaluation of complex interventions forward required an understanding of the system properties giving rise to complexity.

The most successful problem solvers are those whose thinking matches the problem characteristics (Goodman, 2020; Richmond, 1993). To solve systems related problems requires the ability to understand systems.

System Definitions

There are many definitions of a system (Monat & Gannon, 2015). In overhearing me mention that I was getting on a call to discuss systems, my daughter Jenna, age 6, quipped "I know a system. It's something that works all together" (Personal communication, January 23, 2022). In a nutshell that's the basic idea; it isn't "wicked," "super-wicked," a "mess," or even "exotic."

On a more official note, the American Evaluation Association ([AEA], 2018) defines a system as a "set of interrelated elements that interact to achieve an inherent or ascribed purpose" (p. 6). The AEA is never clear that the "system" refers to a complex intervention and that therefore the ascribed purpose refers to the change for which the complex intervention was designed, usually targeting some larger social problem. The failure to differentiate the complex intervention from the complex problem it is intended to solve has created much confusion among those exploring the potential of systems evaluation. We must keep this clear!

The AEA definition is consistent with other system definitions in its reference to elements and that the elements must work together. This is the very definition of complexity. However, the relationship between system elements goes far deeper than just "boxes and arrows" (Checkland, 2000; Williams, 2014). System elements don't just influence each other, they need each other to function: they are interdependent (Brant, 1994). As you will learn in Chapter 5 the interdependence system property underpins the framework for evaluating system efficiency.

The second component of AEA's definition, namely, that system elements work together toward an inherent or ascribed purpose, is also true. However, upon closer examination this aspect of the AEA definition does not accurately capture the idea that system elements work together to create "something" which they cannot achieve independently. That is, *emerging* from the element interdependence is something that none of the system elements possess independently. Ackoff calls the "something" that emerges through the interdependence of system elements the *essential system property*[1] (Brant, 1994). As you will learn in Chapters 5 and 9, the emergent system property has significant implications for evaluating system effectiveness.

To ensure that an evaluation approach is fit for evaluating complex interventions a system definition that more accurately reflects interdependence and emergence is needed. For these reasons, I prefer Ison's (2008) definition of a system as "an integrated whole whose essential properties arise from the relationship [interdependence] between its parts" (p. 142).

System parts, system elements, and system units are interchangeable terms and include a set of plans, resources, authorities, agencies, and their associated human resources (Jackson et al., 2012; Miller, 1978). Basically, a system part is anything needed to make a system work! In Chapter 6 will you learn how to use an understanding of emergence to define a complex interventions' parts and their interdependencies using system actors[2] at all system levels.

Complexity and Systems Properties

Since complexity is defined as something having many moving parts, then by deductive reasoning you might equate interdependence with complexity. I would argue, however, that this reasoning is too simplistic. The property of interdependence suggests an added quality that the term complexity does not capture. For example, it is correct to point out that a clock is complex because it has many moving pieces, but it is qualitatively different to note that all the pieces are dependent on each other to tell time. The property of emergence is also value added in that ascribes a purpose to complexity. It is one thing to say that many pieces make a clock complex, but it is another to say that the purpose of these pieces is to tell time; something that no single piece can do on its own. *Thus, the system properties of interdependence and emergence give complexity quality and purpose, respectively.*

Illustrating the Interdependence and Emergence Properties

Dr. Russel Ackoff, a systems luminary, often used the automobile to illustrate the interdependence and emergence system properties. The essential property of the automobile is to move you from point A to point B. Ackoff pointed out that no single part of an automobile can do that by itself. Neither the motor, transmission, nor wheels can move you by themselves from point A to point B. That is, no single element has the essential system property.

Dr. Russel Ackoff

Ackoff also explained that the automobile parts are interdependent. When the engine, transmission, wheels, and so on work together as intended, the essential system property of the automobile, moving you from point A to point B, emerges. If any part is missing (e.g., the transmission), then the rest of the parts cannot function and the essential system property (i.e., moving from point A to point B) never emerges.

Emergence tells us that a system is *more* than the sum of its part (Meadows, 2008). This, as you will learn in Chapter 9, has important consequences for how we evaluate whether a complex intervention acting as a system is effective. Ackoff described emergence differently, suggesting "a system is not the sum of the behavior of its parts, it is a product of its interactions" (Brant, 1994, 5:19). I like the term "product" better because it emphasizes that the parts cannot simply be added together to understand the essential system property.

A positive customer experience is an example of an emergent property arising from the many interdependent parts in the food service system. No single part can create a positive customer experience and the malfunction or absence of any part decreases the likelihood a positive customer experience will emerge.

I have been criticized at some workshops that the automobile exemplar is oversimplistic and that complex interventions in particular are "wicked," that is, they are more complex than an automobile (Williams & van't Hof, 2016). The system properties of interdependence and emergence hold regardless of intervention complexity. For example, consider something as complex as the U.S. health care system. There are many different perspectives (e.g., patient, medical provider, insurer), as to what the purpose of a health care system might be but, for argument's sake, let us be altruistic and agree that a health care system's essential property is to improve quality of life. There are also many interdependent system parts, such as health care professionals, medical equipment, technology, and the patient that must coordinate to give the health care system its essential property. Importantly, no single health care system element, by itself, can improve the quality of life. Medical equipment, no matter how advanced, is just a piece of equipment without someone trained in its operation. A health professional

Figure 2.1 Georges Seurat's (1884–1886) famous painting *Sunday Afternoon on the Island of La Grande Jatte* is an example of emergence. Seurat used a technique called pointillism in which each of the dots combine to create inspiration. No single dot can create the inspiration, but the dots together can. Steven Sondheim noted that his Broadway musical hit *Sunday in the Park With George* was inspired by Seurat's painting.

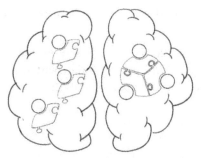

Figure 2.2 Did you know the human brain is actually wired to think like a system? The left side of our brains can detect and understand parts. The right side of our brain is responsible for integrating these parts into an emergent understanding. This explains why those with right-brain injuries can understand sentences but can't synthesize them to understand something like humor (Blake, 2003).

without training and support is just a person. It is the interdependence of the doctor, trained staff, and technology that work together to improve the quality of life; to give the health system its essential property.

In summary, two important system properties that must be considered when tailoring an approach for evaluating complex interventions are interdependence and emergence. It is these properties upon which system evaluation theory rests (Renger, 2015). Further, as von Bertalanffy (1972) stated, "Since the fundamental character of the living thing is its organization, the customary investigation of single parts and processes cannot provide a complete explanation of the vital phenomena" (p. 410). *It is this fact that explains why program evaluation methods grounded in reductionist thinking are ill-equipped to evaluate the interdependence and emergence of complex interventions and why a different approach is needed.*

Recognizing When Your Evaluation Problem Might Require a Systems Approach

To know whether a systems approach is appropriate you must first recognize whether the intervention you are challenged to evaluate is acting as a system. Arnold and Wade (2015) developed a "systems test" which guides the user to determine whether the intervention is acting as a system. The test looks at whether there is a clear purpose (emergent property) and whether there are parts working toward that purpose (interdependence). While this is a good beginning, it is not a diagnostic tool I found useful in scoping out an evaluation strategy with clients.

Donella Meadows (2008), another systems luminary, suggested asking the following questions to differentiate whether you are in fact dealing with a system or "just a bunch of stuff"!:

- "Can you identify parts?"
- "Do the parts affect each other?"
- "Do the parts together produce an effect different from the effect of each part on its own?"

The clients with whom I interact are often unaware that their intervention, that they generically refer to as a program, is operating and functioning as a system. They just do what they do the way they do it and usually do it very well. We also know that evaluators' credibility and client buy-in is impacted by how we communicate: The more jargon and sophisticated terms we use, the less likely anyone will listen to us (Brown et al., 1978). Thus, when first scoping out the evaluation with clients I find it best to avoid using terms like complexity, interdependence, emergence, and for that matter, systems. Instead, I look for clues in the clients' language as to whether their intervention is operating as a system. Cooperation, coalition, collaboration, collective, and coordination (the 5 C's) are mainstream keywords that signal you might be dealing with a system. These keywords often indicate there are many interdependent parts working together to achieve something greater than they could independently.

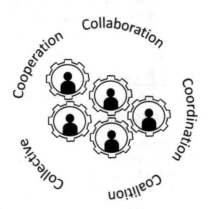

For example, I evaluated numerous emergency management (EM) preparedness exercises as well as the COVID-19 response for a county health department. The goal of EM is to save lives and property (FEMA, 2019). The EM literature repeatedly emphasizes the need for agencies to collaborate and coordinate to achieve this goal (FEMA, 2007). In the COVID-19 response, public health, law enforcement, first responders, EM, private businesses, the media, and volunteer organizations like the Red Cross were parts of a complex intervention needing to collaborate and coordinate to save lives (FEMA, 2008). The EM system is a complex intervention in which no single agency can achieve the essential property of saving lives by themselves and the absence of any one agency jeopardizes the system's essential property from emerging. In short, saving property and lives emerges through the responding agencies' interdependence.

The federal guidance for evaluating EM response focuses on assessing the extent to which individuals and agencies have the needed response capabilities (e.g., know how to administer a swab test, can use a ventilator, have volunteers with specific capabilities, etc.; FEMA, 2011, 2020). That is, the FEMA evaluation guidance is focused on individual puzzle pieces. However, the continual reference to collaboration and coordination acted as clues for me to start evaluating the EM response as the system it was intended to be rather than individual parts (Renger, 2021).

> As you will learn in the final chapter, one barrier to evaluation use is the perception that systems evaluators are elitist and systems thinking is difficult. Therefore, to improve evaluation report utility I deliberately use the 5 C's when making recommendations rather than referencing interdependence and/or an emergent system property.

Types of Systems

Scholars use different criteria to classify systems. For example, Gharajedaghi and Ackoff (1984) defined four types of systems differentiated by whether the parts and the whole have choice and therefore a purpose: deterministic, ecological, animate, and social. The *Encyclopedia of Management* (Gale Publishing, 2012) defines three systems types: mechanical, biological, and social. Although, as you will learn in Chapter 5, my journey in systems evaluation began by hiring a biologist to help me understand systems, my focus has been on evaluating complex interventions in social systems. A *social system* is "a patterned series of interrelationships existing between individuals, groups, and institutions forming a coherent whole" (Merriam-Webster, n.d.). This definition aligns nicely with that of Ison (2008), placing emphasis on the human nature of the systems parts.

Social systems, and by extension the complex interventions operating within them, are open systems (McGill et al., 2020). An open system is defined as "systems that interact with other systems or the outside environment" (Gale Publishing, 2012, p. 734). Complex interventions operating as systems are also by definition complex adaptive systems ([CAS]; Carmichael & Hadžikadić, 2019; Holland, 1992). "A CAS is a collection of individual nodes [i.e., parts, elements, agents] that self-organize and ex-change information amongst each other locally to produce spontaneous and emergent global outcomes" (Davis & Stroink, 2016, p. 576). As noted above, complexity is an inherent characteristic of a system, thus, for me the terms CAS and systems are redundant. Therefore, for this book's purpose, the terms system and CAS are interchangeable.

In contrast, a closed system "has very little [or no] interaction with the other systems and the outside environment" (Zhang & Ahmed, 2020, p. 422). Closed systems tend to become less predictable, chaotic, disordered, and uncertain, a principle known as entropy (Miller, 1978).

Illustrating Open Versus Closed Systems: COVID-19

In the evaluation of the pandemic response, I used my systems thinking skills to correctly *predict* that complex interventions acting as open systems would become closed systems (Renger, 2021). Emergency response systems are complex interventions designed to be open systems, depending on outside resources as the scope of the emergency grows. For example, in a wildfire, local resources are brought to bear first. If the wildfire becomes too large, then additional support is requested from the county. If the wildfire continues to grow, then state and federal support might be requested. However, the pandemic's limitless boundaries, hence the name pandemic, meant that surrounding systems that normally could have provided outside assistance were themselves dealing with the same emergency. Thus, local emergency response systems were left to fend for themselves; they were going into shock and becoming closed systems. The failure to recognize this as the pandemic was unfolding meant valuable time was lost in securing personal protective equipment (PPE) locally. The entropy, the chaos, that ensued was predictable (Miller, 1978) and was evidenced by hoarding of PPE, jumping vaccination lines, and so on.

Pre COVID-19: An Open System   COVID-19: A Closed System

Soft Systems Versus Hard Systems

The term soft system refers to a specific inquiry method to make sense of the world's complexities (Checkland, 2000). It has been dubbed "soft" because of its emphasis of systems thinking as a *learning process* (Checkland, 2000). For our intents and purposes, soft systems and systems thinking are interchangeable terms.

Alternatively, hard systems, refers to the complex intervention being evaluated, its construction, its processes, and its operation. A hard system is the complex intervention and the object of the evaluation. Thus, for our intents and purposes the terms system and hard system are interchangeable, both referring to the complex intervention being evaluated. In this book you will learn how to apply systems thinking (i.e., soft system skills) to define and evaluate complex interventions acting as systems (i.e., hard systems).

Conclusion

In this chapter you learned that systems are inherently complex. It has been my experience that many evaluators treat complexity as "a bunch of stuff." As such they have no standard by which to evaluate complexity and are often overwhelmed, hence referring to the problem as "wicked." It is my contention that viewing complexity from a systems perspective allows evaluators to exploit an understanding of system properties to define an operational (interdependence) and functional (emergence) purpose of complexity. That is, when we evaluate complex interventions using a system lens, we are considering how complexity is organized and to what end.

Notes

1. Throughout the book I use the term essential system property and emergent system property interchangeably.
2. System actors is an all-encompassing term that includes all those responsible for implementing a complex intervention acting as a system (e.g., leaders, staff).

References

American Evaluation Association. (2018). *Principles for effective use of systems thinking in evaluation*. Systems in Evaluation TIG. https://www.aes .asn.au/images/stories/regions/QLD/SETIG-Principles-FINAL-DRAFT -2018-9-9.pdf

Arnold, R. D., & Wade, J. P. (2015). A definition of systems thinking: A systems approach. *Procedia Computer Science, 44*, 669–678. https://doi .org/10.1016/j.procs.2015.03.050

Blake, M. L. (2003). Affective language and humor appreciation after right hemisphere brain damage. *Seminars in Speech and Language, 24*(2), 107–120. https://doi.org/10.1055/s-2003-38902

Brant, S. (1994). *If Russ Ackoff had given a TED talk* [Video]. YouTube. https://www.youtube.com/watch?v=OqEeIG8aPPk

Brown, R. D., & Braskamp, L. A., & Newman, D. L. (1978). Evaluator credibility as a function of report style: Do jargon and data make a difference? *American Educational Research Journal, 15*(3), 441–450. https:// doi.org/10.1177/0193841X7800200209

Carmichael T., & Hadžikadić, M. (2019). The fundamentals of complex adaptive systems. In T. Carmichael, A. Collins, & M. Hadžikadić (Eds.), *Complex adaptive systems: Understanding complex systems* (pp. 1–16). Springer. https://doi.org/10.1007/978-3-030-20309-2_1

Checkland, P. (2000). Soft systems methodology: A thirty-year retrospective. *Systems Research and Behavioral Science, 17*, 11–58.

Davis, A. C., & Stroink, M. L. (2016). The relationship between systems thinking and the new ecological paradigm. *Systems Research and Behavioral Science, 33*(4), 575–586. https://doi.org/10.1002/sres.2371

Federal Emergency Management Agency. (2007). *Principles of emergency management*. https://training.fema.gov/hiedu/emprinciples.aspx

Federal Emergency Management Agency. (2008). *Emergency support function annexes: An introduction*. https://www.fema.gov/pdf/emergency/ nrf/nrf-annexes-all.pdf

Federal Emergency Management Agency. (2011). *Crosswalk of target capabilities to core capabilities*. https://www.fema.gov/pdf/prepared/ crosswalk.pdf

Federal Emergency Management Agency. (2019). *2019 national threat and hazard identification and risk assessment (THIRA)*. https://www.fema

.gov/sites/default/files/2020-06/fema_national-thira-overview
-methodology_2019_0.pdf

Federal Emergency Management Agency. (2020). *Homeland security and exercise evaluation program (HSEEP).* https://www.fema.gov/sites/default/files/2020-04/Homeland-Security-Exercise-and-Evaluation-Program-Doctrine-2020-Revision-2-2-25.pdf

Gale Publishing. (2012). Open and closed systems. In *Encyclopedia of Management* (7th ed.; pp. 734–736).

Gharajedaghi, J., & Ackoff, R. L. (1984). Mechanisms, organisms and social systems. *Strategic Management Journal, 5*(3), 289–300. http://www.jstor.org/stable/2486282

Goodman, M. (2020). *Systems thinking: What, why, when, where and how?* The Systems Thinker. https://thesystemsthinker.com/systems-thinking-what-why-when-where-and-how/

Holland, J. H. (1992). Complex adaptive systems. *Daedalus, 121*(1), 17–30. http://www.jstor.org/stable/20025416

Ison, R. L. (2008). Systems thinking and practice for action research. In P. W. Reason, & H. Bradbury (Eds.), *The SAGE handbook of action research participative inquiry and practice* (2nd ed.; pp. 139–158.). SAGE Publications.

Jackson, B. A., Faith, K. S., & Willis, H. H. (2012). Evaluating the reliability of emergency response systems for large-scale incident operations. *Rand Health Quarterly, 2*(3), 8. https://www.ncbi.nlm.nih.gov/pmc/articles/PMC4945240/

McGill, E., Marks, D., Er, V., Penney, T., Petticrew, M., & Egan, M. (2020). Qualitative process evaluation from a complex system perspective: A systematic review and framework for public health evaluators. *PLoS Med, 17*(11), e1003368. https://doi.org/10.1371/journal.pmed.1003368

Meadows, D. (2008). *Thinking in systems: A primer.* Chelsea Green Publishing.

Merriam-Webster. (n.d.). Social system. In, *Merriam-Webster.com dictionary.* https://www.merriam-webster.com/dictionary/social%20system

Miller, J. G. (1978). *Living systems: The basic concepts.* https://www.panarchy.org/miller/livingsystems.html#Anchor-11-6296

Monat, J. P., & Gannon, T. F. (2015). What is systems thinking? A review of selected literature plus recommendations. *American Journal of Systems Science, 4*(1), 11–26.

Renger, R. (2015). System evaluation theory (SET). *Evaluation Journal of Australasia, 15*(4), 16–28. https://doi.org/10.1177/1035719X1501500403

Renger, R. (2021). COVID-19: Exposing the need for emergency management to invest in systems thinking. *Journal of Emergency Management, 19*(7), 39–48. https://doi.org/10.5055/jem.0607

Richmond, B. (1993). Systems thinking: Critical thinking skills for the 1990s and beyond. *System Dynamics Review, 9*(2), 113–133. https://doi.org/10.1002/sdr.4260090203

Seurat, G. (1884–1886). *A Sunday afternoon on the Island of La Grande Jatte* [Painting]. Art Institute of Chicago, Chicago, IL, United States. https://www.artic.edu/artworks/61616/oil-sketch-for-a-sunday-on-la -grande-jatte-1884

Von Bertalanffy, L. (1972). The history and status of general systems theory. *The Academy of Management Journal, 15*(4), 407–426. www.jstor.org/stable/255139

Williams, B. (2014). *Week 36: Systems thinking.* Better Evaluation. https://www.betterevaluation.org/en/blog/systems_thinking

Williams, B., & van 't Hof. (2016). *Wicked solutions: A systems approach to wicked problems* (2nd ed.). Bob Williams.

Zhang, B. H., & Ahmed, S. A. M. (2020). Systems thinking—Ludwig Von Bertalanffy, Peter Senge, and Donella Meadows. In B. Akpan & T. J. Kennedy (Eds.), *Science Education in Theory and Practice* (pp. 419–436). https://doi.org/10.1007/978-3-030-43620-9_28

3

System Boundaries, Levels, and Subsystems

Good evaluators need to know their boundaries.

In Chapter 2 you learned about two essential system properties, interdependence and emergence, that provide a path forward for evaluating complex interventions acting as systems. While there is often considerable disagreement among evaluators on most topics, there is universal agreement that the starting point for any evaluation is to define the evaluand (Davidson, 2005). Our goal in defining a complex intervention acting as a system is to define its system properties. However, to be able to define interdependence and the essential system property that emerges from that interdependence, you first need to define the system parts. Once you know the system parts, then you can define how they work together. In this chapter you will learn why the boundary principle and understanding of system levels is important in identifying the system parts to be included in the evaluation.

System Evaluation Theory, pages 35–54
Copyright © 2022 by Information Age Publishing
www.infoagepub.com
All rights of reproduction in any form reserved.

There is a difference between a system property and a system principle. A *property* "is an attribute or characteristic of something." A *principle* is "a proposition or value that is a guide for behavior or evaluation" ("Principle," 2021). I like this definition of a principle because of its emphasis on evaluation utility. In evaluating complex interventions acting as systems, we must first define the system properties and then apply the systems principles to evaluate whether the intervention is meeting its operational (i.e., efficiency) and functional (i.e., effectiveness) purpose.

The Boundary Principle

A system boundary separates the created system from its environment.
—Wolski, 2020

Where to draw a boundary around a system depends on the purpose of the discussion.
—Meadows, 2008, p. 91

A system boundary demarks where a system starts and ends. As applied to evaluation, it is the parts that do/do not comprise the complex intervention acting as a system. When we demarcate system boundaries for evaluation purposes, we must recognize the boundaries we draw are artificial, created out of necessity to deal with the realities of time and resources. The challenge is to evaluate the interdependencies within the boundary we establish for evaluation purposes as they actually occur (Checkland, 2000). In Chapter 6 you will learn a 7-step method designed to capture, as accurately as possible, the complex intervention system structure and processes so that you can have confidence that the evaluation of interdependencies is meaningful.

In my experience, defining the boundaries of a complex intervention acting as a system is best accomplished using a bottom-up rather than top–down approach. This organic approach works best by first understanding the system's (i.e., complex intervention) emergent property. If you first establish a common understanding of a system's emergent property, then you can identify who or what shares that purpose, that is the system parts. In turn, knowing the system parts that are aligned to the emergent property gives you an initial skeleton, or system boundary.

Establishing the criteria for setting boundaries with a client is as much art as it is science. When working with a client remember that systems terminology, like boundaries, can be off-putting and create unnecessary barriers with clients. Try using a term like "bookends" to help explain the boundaries principle to clients.

Although I recommend using the emergent property as the initial criterion for establishing system boundaries, additional criteria may be needed to further refine the boundaries of the complex intervention. The criteria you choose, in my experience, are idiosyncratic and dependent on the context. For example, when I evaluated a regional center for translational research, a complex intervention, the emergent system property was researcher self-efficacy. In defining the boundaries, we considered all the agencies and institutions that could contribute to the emergent system property that fell within specific geographical boundaries (i.e., the Dakotas) and additional substantive boundaries imposed by the funder (i.e., cancer-specific research; DaCCoTA, 2021).

In another evaluation I conducted of cancer screening services, the emergent system property was quality patient care. The system boundaries for that complex intervention were defined by health service providers delivering services to a targeted patient population (i.e., uninsured or underinsured women).

In evaluating a cardiac care system, the boundaries were defined by those agencies who needed to work together to achieve a positive patient outcome (i.e., the emergent system property) beginning with a trigger event (i.e., call to 911) and ending with the patient arriving at a definitive care center (i.e., a time criterion).

Implications of the Boundary Principle on Evaluation Practice

I am often asked: "How much will it [the evaluation] cost?" Demarcating the boundaries of a complex intervention acting as a system is important in understanding the evaluation scope and estimating the evaluation cost (McGill et al., 2020; Yarbrough et al., 2010). Thus, the broader the boundaries, the larger the scale, the more parts, the more interdependencies, and the more stakeholder perspectives need to be included. System evaluation theory is heavily dependent on stakeholder involvement which adds time and cost.

Recall that "perspectives" is one of the "big three" system thinking notions (Chapter 1) embraced in evaluation (Williams & van 't Hof, 2016). Perspectives are always operating and embedded in every aspect of SET and system evaluation. As you will learn in the chapters to come, the success of SET depends on drawing on the perspectives of system actors at different system levels to define and evaluate the complex intervention acting as a system.

The larger scale does not, however, change the approach to evaluating complex interventions acting as systems. A larger scale likely, but not necessarily, means more work. This is because as the boundary expands there may be more parts, and additional structures and processes to consider. In Chapter 6 you will learn a method, called process flow mapping (PFM) for defining system processes. The method for defining these processes does not change as the scale grows, but the time it takes to define them might.

Scale for evaluation purposes refers to the number of system parts and interdependencies. As you broaden the boundaries of a complex intervention acting as a system the scale is said to increase. As the boundaries increase so might the number of parts, interdependencies, and perspectives needing to be considered in the evaluation.

Subsystems and System Levels (Overview)

Since, as Meadows (2008) noted, the world is one big system, then whatever boundaries you create for evaluation purposes will, by definition, be a subsystem. The idea of subsystems is certainly not new. For example, one of the most widely cited models for explaining human development, Bronfenbrenner's (1974, 1977) ecological model, is steeped in an understanding of the interaction between system levels, or layers. While evaluators may not necessarily be concerned with explaining human behavior, an understanding of subsystems is important for understanding what to evaluate and, as you will learn in Chapter 10, how to derive possible recommendations for system improvements.

The natural world is often used as a metaphor to better understand systems and their components. This should come as no surprise because of the extensive use of systems theory in the natural sciences (Burnes, 2005). For example, Miller (1978) defined seven subsystems, using living systems as a boundary criterion (see Figure 3.1). Those studying and evaluating organizations, such as the Haines Institute, have found great utility in applying the living system boundary criteria to studying interdependence and emergence in organizations, teams, and individuals ("Approaching Business With Systems Thinking," n.d.).

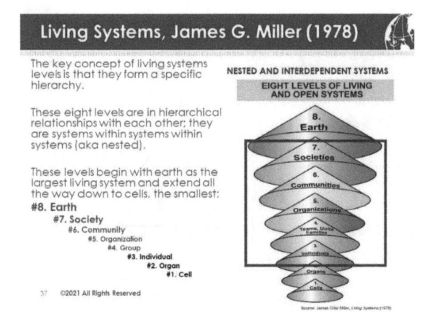

Figure 3.1 Borrowed with permission from the Haines Institute (www.haines centre.com).

Subsystems and System Levels as Applied to Evaluating Complex Interventions Acting as Systems

The number of criteria you apply to establish the boundaries of a complex intervention acting as a system is not preordained. However, with each boundary criterion you apply, you essentially create, or carve out, another, smaller, interconnected subsystem. For example, when I was evaluating a cancer screening program, the boundary was initially based on the emergent property of patient care and the additional funder criterion of client eligibility. This resulted in a boundary consisting of 14 contractors serving uninsured/underinsured women in the state of Arizona. The client overseeing the complex intervention acting as a system, the Arizona Department of Health Services, explained that they wanted to understand problems with the data collection and reporting mechanisms within the defined boundaries. Applying this criterion created an additional subsystem that began at the first point a contractor collected patient data required for reporting purposes and ended when the contractor data was uploaded, collated, and sent to the federal agency sponsoring the initiative (see Figure 3.2).

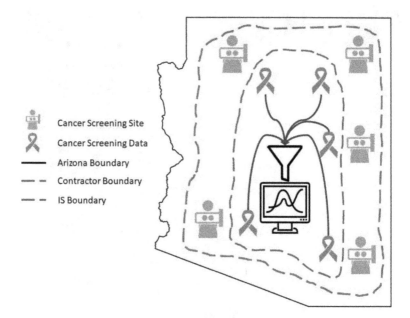

Cancer Screening Site

Cancer Screening Data

Arizona Boundary

Contractor Boundary

IS Boundary

Figure 3.2 The subsystems of the ADHS evaluation.

Subsystems Mirror the Systems in Which They Are Embedded: Fractal Theory

As we continue to create subsystems by applying boundary criteria, there is an important feature about the relationship between the subsystems being carved out that impacts the evaluation of system interdependence and emergence. Mandelbrot noted that in nature subsystems are essentially a "fraction" of the larger system, hence, the name fractal theory (TED, 2010). Once again, the measuring cup metaphor works well here. He observed that the smallest parts of cauliflower, mountains, leaves, and clouds all resembled the whole cauliflower, mountain, leaf, and cloud, respectively. In his words, "Each part is like the whole, but smaller. And, he was able to prove these relationships mathematically!

Mandelbrot's theory was derived from his observations of nature, but they also apply to evaluating complex interventions acting as systems. For example, during the COVID-19 pandemic we witnessed the same inequity in vaccine distribution (i.e., the complex intervention) occurring at multiple system levels (WHO, 2021). Poorer, mostly non-White, communities within the Arizona municipalities couldn't get access to the vaccine when it first became available. The exact same scenario played out at the state level, with poorer counties, like those upon which tribal lands are located, not getting access to early vaccine doses. The same set of circumstances played out at the national level, where poorer states with large Black, Indigenous, and people of color populations had less vaccine access than predominantly White states. Finally, at an international level there were considerable inequities between richer, predominately White (e.g., United States and Commonwealth) and poorer countries.

Friedman's (2005) results-based accountability method is anchored in the idea of subsystems and fractal theory. Friedman (2005) noted that "it is possible to view social structures through this [fractal] lens and see government bureaucracies and social networks as fractal entities with similar characteristics and structures at progressively larger and smaller levels of magnification" (p. 147). For example, Friedman noted the city government has the same structure as the state government which mirrors the federal government. Thus, by extension the evaluation approach used at one level should be applicable at another level! In Chapter 9 you will learn more about the implications of fractal theory and its implications for determining who is responsible for the system level responsible for evaluating emergence.

In the evaluation and system literature the terms subsystems, levels, system levels, fractals, and nested systems are used interchangeably. The Russian doll metaphor is often used to explain these concepts. However, there are many such metaphors. The metaphor I like to represent system layers in evaluation are the measuring cups. The parallel between measuring and evaluation is more intuitive. Regardless of level, each cup serves the same purpose.

Application of the Boundary, Subsystem, and Fractal System Principles

Consistent with systems thinking, it should come as no surprise that the interdependence and emergence system properties, boundary principle, and fractal theory are themselves interconnected. As an educator I was challenged to find a way to explain the relationships between these systems ideas to a general audience with diverse backgrounds. I needed an example that was easy to understand and did not require substantive content expertise. Using an example from the systems (i.e., complex interventions) with which I was most familiar, such as emergency management and health care, would likely mean that most of my audience would not be able to relate and those who did have content expertise may miss the larger points as they argue over unimportant minutiae. Therefore, I am sharing with you my solution to this problem using a field trip to the Mall of America at the 2019 AEA annual evaluation conference in Minneapolis as a case study. Please keep in mind that what I describe below was my teaching strategy for explaining different system properties and principles, it is *not* the evaluation strategy, namely SET, you will learn about in later chapters for defining and evaluating a system.

The field trip began by observing *a single fast-food restaurant* located inside the mall, inside a food court, in this case a Subway™. For the purpose of this example, consider the Subway™ to be an intervention. Our first task was to ascertain whether the Subway was in fact acting as a system, or whether it was just a bunch of stuff (Meadows, 2008). To do this we first identified all the restaurant system parts. Recall from Chapter 2 that system parts include a set of plans, resources, authorities, agencies, and their associated human resources (Jackson et al., 2012). We noted 11 system parts including the manager, line staff, cashiers, equipment, and suppliers. We also noted there had to be the right mix and balance of parts. For example, all the front-line staff needed people skills, but the skills required to work with suppliers, prepare food, take an order, execute an order, and complete the transaction were different. Staff with only one skill type wouldn't be able to work effectively within the system, thus enough staff needed to be cross-trained in other skills (e.g., making sandwiches).

We also reasoned the Subway system parts were interdependent, noting the essential system property, which we defined as a positive customer experience, could only emerge through the interdependence of these parts. To test our interdependence and emergence assumptions we considered what would happen if even one system part was missing. For example, if the oven did not function, then there would be no fresh bread or if a staff member failed to report for work, then it might stress the system. It seemed any missing part directly impacted the other parts from functioning and compromised the emergence of the essential system property (i.e., a positive customer experience). By going through this process, we essentially answered the questions that Meadows (2008) suggested be used to determine whether we just had "a bunch of stuff" or "a system" (see Chapter 2). The presence of interdependent parts and an emergent property led us to conclude the Subway was operating as a system.

Having decided that the Subway was operating as a system we then embarked on demarcating the system boundaries, where the Subway system started and stopped. The criterion we used to create our system for evaluation purposes were the physical borders of the restaurant. However, from Figure 3.3 you can see that the system could easily be extended past the physical store boundaries to the supplier, like the farmers that grow the produce needed for the sandwich toppings. It is my position, and one shared by Ison (2008), that where the boundary starts and stops is up to the client. In Chapter 6 you will learn how to guide the client to define the boundary criteria and establish the system boundaries.

We then roughly plotted how we thought the parts might work together. We depicted these relationships by using connecting arrows (see Figure 3.3). Of course, in reality connecting system parts with arrows would be done with those who have substantive content expertise (Ison, 2008; Renger et al., 2017); namely, the staff and managers.

We then explored what type of evaluation questions we could answer vis-à-vis the interdependence of system parts. Most of the questions related to the interactions between staff and between staff and the equipment needed to ensure customer satisfaction. For example, "Was the customer's order being correctly relayed from the greeter, to toppings, to the cashier? Was the cooking and cooling equipment required to ensure quality sandwiches regularly inspected and functional?" It was our observation that these questions were more targeted and meaningful than a typical program evaluation, such as, "How well was the service delivered?" This, in turn, could lead to more actionable evaluation recommendations.

One of the workshop participants astutely noted the connecting arrows in Figure 3.3 only superficially represented the interdependence of system parts. She observed that there was much more happening

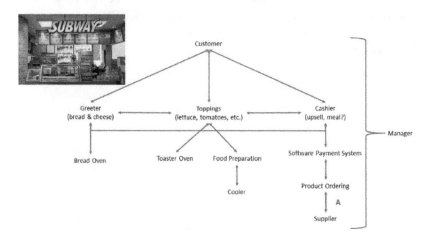

Figure 3.3 The interdependent system parts of a fast-food restaurant.

"inside" each of the connecting arrows. This is very important. Too often I have observed people simply connecting boxes and arguing they now have a system. As Williams (2014) wrote, "Evaluators generally worry and argue about what's in the boxes and tend to ignore the arrows between them" (n.p.). The connecting arrows have meaning!

I refer to understanding what is happening inside an arrow as "unpacking the arrow." I use a technique called PFM to unpack the arrow; that is, to develop the detail that each arrow represents (Renger et al., 2016).

In writing this book I called on the help of a friend of mine, Jay Moulten, an entrepreneur in the food service industry to help unpack just one of the arrows shown in Figure 3.3, labeled with a red A, as per the PFM technique. The result of that exercise is shown in Figure 3.4.

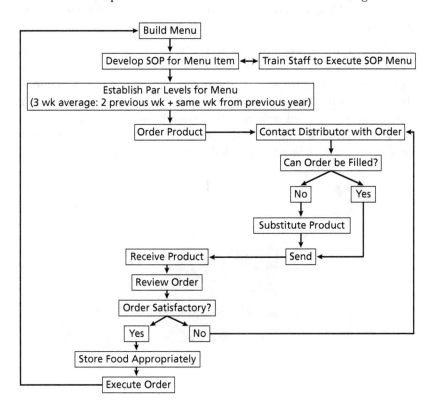

Figure 3.4 Unpacking the arrow: Detailing the process depicted by arrow A in Figure 3.3.

This level of detail is needed to confirm and understand the nature of the interdependence of system parts. It also serves as the standard of acceptability against which you can evaluate whether the system is meeting its operational purpose, that is its efficiency (Green et al., 1980). Put another way, to evaluate whether the system parts are working together as they *should* you first need to know how they are *supposed* to work together. Once this detail is documented, you'll need to refer to Chapter 7 to learn how to apply several additional system principles to evaluate different types of interdependencies and whether the system parts are coordinating as intended.

To illustrate system levels, we engaged in a synthesis process thus defining the higher-level system within which the fast-food restaurant was embedded. To do this we broadened the physical boundaries *to include all the fast-food restaurants within the mall food court*. Again for illustration purposes consider the food-court to be the complex intervention. Figure 3.5 shows how the fast-food restaurant is embedded within the food court.

We used the same approach to verify whether the food court was behaving as a system as we did with the Subway restaurant. We reasoned the essential property of the food court system was the same as the Subway: a positive customer experience. We reasoned this essential system property would only emerge through the interdependence of the food court restaurants. At this system level a proper mix and balance of system parts was also needed for the emergence of the essential

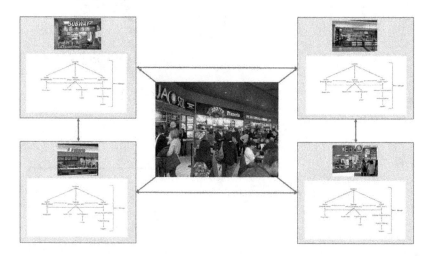

Figure 3.5   The fast-food restaurant embedded in the food court system.

system property. For example, consider a family coming to the food court, each with different tastes and/or dietary restrictions. If one of the family member's dietary needs cannot be met, then the customer experience is likely to be negative and the family may choose to eat elsewhere or not return again. "Can you imagine a food court that just serves burgers?!" In other words, there is an ideal mix and balance of interdependent restaurants needed to create and sustain the essential system property.

This first level of synthesis illustrated several important points regarding the influence that broadening the boundaries has on evaluating systems. First, regarding emergence, even though the boundaries broadened, the essential system property remained the same.

Second, the system parts, qualitatively changed from individual components of the Subway to the food court restaurants themselves. The number of interdependencies needing to be evaluated is directly tied to the number of food court restaurants. Our initial supposition was that evaluating a higher system level was going to require more evaluation resources. Whether this supposition was true depended on the relative number of system parts defined at each level. Our Subway level evaluation consisted of 11 parts. If the number of restaurants exceeded 11, then there would be more interdependencies to evaluate. However, if the number of food court restaurants was less than 11, then evaluating the higher system level would be less resource intensive!

Third, the *nature* of the interdependency-related evaluation questions is dictated by the system level and the parts that define them. At the lower level, the interdependencies are between staff, clients, and equipment within the Subway. The evaluation of interdependencies might focus on the extent to which information is efficiently exchanged between line staff. For example, from the person taking the order, to the person adding toppings, to the cashier. At the food court, or next highest system level, the interdependencies are between the different restaurants. At this level the evaluation might focus on the extent to which all restaurants in the food court abide by the Hazard Analysis Critical Control Point principles (Food and Drug Administration, 2017). If just one restaurant was noncompliant with food safety measures, for example via a cockroach infestation, this would have immediate consequences for all food court restaurants. The local health department would automatically inspect all restaurants for the infestation, possibly having to shut down several restaurants. The closure of one or several of the food court restaurants for health reasons would impact consumer confidence in all restaurants.

To further validate our observations about the relationship between expanding boundaries, interdependence, and emergence we again engaged in synthesis by further expanding the physical boundaries *to include all businesses within the Mall of America.* As shown in Figure 3.6, the system parts we identified were now business clusters. We then reasoned that the clusters themselves were interdependent. Again, for illustration purposes consider the business clusters to be the complex intervention. A variety of business clusters are needed to attract customers to the mall to ensure everyone who visits will have a positive customer experience. Attractions are necessary for families with children. Retail outlets are needed to meet the clothing needs of women, men, and children. Food establishments of all types are needed to meet the idiosyncratic needs of shoppers. Just imagine a typical day at the mall, you walk around, you look at different stores, you get hungry, then you enjoy some entertainment, then you might like a coffee, and so on. If any part was missing, then the positive customer experience would be less likely to emerge.

If you doubt the interdependence of businesses, then consider the impact of so-called "anchor stores" on the mall systems. The research clearly shows small mall businesses revenue depends on the customer traffic that anchor stores attract (Damian et al., 2011; NPR Staff, 2020). Anchor stores, typically retail stores, are collapsing because of the shift to online shopping (Thomas, 2020). People don't visit these anchor

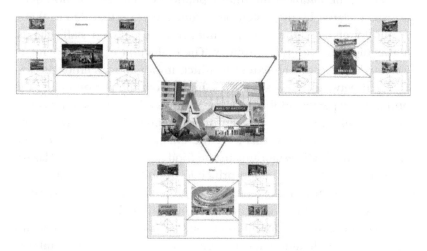

Figure 3.6 Business subsystems operating within the Mall of America.

stores because they can get what they need delivered to their door. Less mall traffic means less food court traffic. Less food court traffic means restaurants with smaller margins (e.g., those catering to unique diets) are likely to go under. This decreases the stability of the food court and this then cycles back to people not wanting to come to the mall.

In terms of emergence, the essential system property at the mall level is the same as the previous two subsystem levels. *Thus, no matter what level of the system (i.e., the complex intervention) you are carving out, or creating, for evaluation purposes the emergent system property is the same.*

As we expanded the physical boundaries to the mall level, we again observed that increasing the scale did not necessarily mean a greater resource burden in terms of defining and evaluating interdependencies. In our example, the system parts at the highest level (i.e., three business clusters) were less than the lower level (i.e., four food court restaurants), which was less than the lowest system level (i.e., 11 Subway staff and equipment). So, in fact as we moved up system levels, the number of interdependencies needing to be evaluated decreased. It has been my experience that generally speaking as the intervention scale size increases, the number of interdependencies increases. However, this may not always be the case because what constitutes a system part may change as you move up or down system levels.

Third, the nature of the evaluation questions at this higher level provides qualitatively different insights as to what constitutes a positive customer experience than those at lower system levels. For example, "What is the timing of the opening/closing of these three clusters of businesses that optimizes a positive customer experience?"

We also observed the fractal principle operating at the mall level. We looked at a mall schematic and saw how the mall was partitioned into four segments: North, South, East and West. Each segment had an anchor store. Each had a large chain coffee store. Within each subsystem the concept of mix and balance was again operating. For example, the mix and balance of retail stores was about the same in each quadrant: there were more women's clothing shops, but the number of women's shops in each mall segment was roughly the same. Attractions were centralized, so that they contributed equally to all four mall segments.

The boundary principle and notion of system levels has important implications for how we evaluate interventions. It does not matter whether an intervention is labeled as a project, program, strategy, activity, policy, or system. The determining factor in deciding whether a system evaluation approach is appropriate is whether the parts of the intervention are operating and functioning as a system. Interventions operating as systems will differ in their level of complexity. It is errant to assume an intervention labeled as a program is necessarily less complex than an intervention labeled as a system. The evaluation must demarcate the boundaries of the intervention for evaluation purposes and define the appropriate interdependencies needing to be evaluated for that system level.

Implications of Fractal Theory on Evaluating Systems: The Check-Mix Rule

When I first learned about fractal theory, I started down a path of examining whether all the mall subsystems could be linked by an actual mathematical, fraction-type, formula. I learned businesses and urban planners are very deliberate in using data to drive store locations (Frankhauser, 2015; Max, 2019). I also learned businesses often decide where to locate their store simply based on the location of one of the big chains in their industry, explaining why so many Burger King and McDonalds restaurants can be found near each other. This is an example of a simple, order generating rule (Burnes, 2005; Foster-Fishman & Watson, 2011). Simple, order generating rules can often underlie what appears to be complex system behavior (Burnes, 2005). For example, scientists have noted that fish and birds obey three simple rules (avoid colliding with your immediate neighbor, move in the direction of the group, and be attracted to your own kind) that enable them to create incredibly complex formations without colliding (Frederick, 1998; Friederici, 2009). We will revisit the power of using simple, order generating rules as recommendations for improving the efficiency of complex interventions acting as systems in Chapter 10.

It seemed logical to believe that if I was persistent, had time, and the substantive content and mathematical expertise, then I could define an underlying mall fractal formula. However, I concluded that while it was a nice theoretical exercise, as a practitioner this was, well, just not practical! I just couldn't imagine my clients having the time, willingness, and resources to pay me to define an underlying fractal formula for evaluation purposes.

So, I began to wonder how I could practically apply fractal theory in evaluating complex interventions acting as systems. Then one evening as I was watching my favorite NFL team, the New England Patriots play I was munching on some Chex-Mix™. As I looked into the bowl, it struck me that the mix itself was also fractal. From a distance you could see all the bits and pieces. And every handful, no matter how large, always seemed to maintain roughly the same mix and balance of bits and pieces. I began thinking about the mall example and reasoned that every system level needed to be concerned about getting the right mix and balance of parts. I then started thinking about every complex intervention I knew like transportation, health, emergency management, and so on. It seemed across all these system types it was important to have the right mix and balance of parts. The incorrect proportion of trains to planes to cars to taxis to boats in a public transportation system would cause major system inefficiencies and reduce the likelihood that the system's essential property of moving people from point A to point B would emerge. Similarly, the incorrect mix of hospitals, health care professionals, emergency medical services, and medical equipment in a health care system would have disastrous effects on prolonging life. I came to realize that as an evaluator I needed to intentionally engage content experts, especially if I was helping in the design phases of a complex intervention, to define the correct mix and balance of system parts. Based on fractal theory I modified my approach for defining complex interventions acting as systems by adding a rule I call "check-mix," essentially asking stakeholders to consider whether the mix and balance of system parts is correct. You will learn how to apply this rule in Chapter 6 when learning the steps in defining a system.

Chex-Mix is an example of fractal theory that spawned
the Renger Check-Mix Rule

As you will learn in Chapter 6, I recommend using experts to demarcate the boundaries of a complex intervention acting as a system and to define the system parts. However, as I reflected on my evaluations of chronic disease coalitions, I recall numerous times when these coalitions failed. Often the resources of multiple agencies were needed to address an issue, but the coalition strategy was to make sure there were no overlapping or competing agencies and that every community need was represented by one agency at the table. There was perhaps the right mix, but not the right balance! Had I been a systems thinker, I would have been better equipped to challenge coalitions regarding the mix and balance of their members.

Conclusion

The evaluation of a complex intervention acting as a system begins by establishing the system boundaries. In my experience, it is best to let the system boundary emerge from the process of defining its parts. You will learn how to engage system stakeholders in this bottom–up approach in Chapter 6.

Understanding system levels has three important implications for evaluation. First, the emergent system property, central to evaluating whether a system meets its functional purpose (i.e., effectiveness) remains the same across system levels. Second, what constitutes system parts changes at each system level. At each level you are evaluating interdependencies, but the evaluation questions are qualitatively different. Finally, as you will learn in Chapter 10, understanding system levels is important for deriving improvement recommendations. That is, often the solution for the inefficiencies of a complex intervention at one level can only be solved by engaging the next higher level.

References

Approaching Business With Systems Thinking. (n.d.). Haines Centre for Strategic Management. https://www.hainescentre.com/articles/systems-thinking/

Bronfenbrenner, U. (1974). Developmental research, public policy, and the ecology of childhood. *Child Development, 45*(1), 1–5. https://www.jstor.org/stable/1127743

Bronfenbrenner, U. (1977). Toward an experimental ecology of human development. *American Psychologist, 32*(7), 513–531. https://doi.org/10.1037/0003-066X.32.7.513

Burnes, B. (2005). Complexity theory and organizational change. *International Journal of Management Reviews, 7*(2), 73–90. https://doi.org/10.1111/j.1468-2370.2005.00107.x

Checkland, P. (2000). Soft systems methodology: A thirty-year retrospective. *Systems Research and Behavioral Science, 17*, S11–S58.

DaCCoTA. (2021). *Dakota cancer collaborative on translational activity.* University of North Dakota. https://med.und.edu/daccota/

Damian, D. S., Curto, J. D., & Pinto, J. C. (2011). The impact of anchor stores on the performance of shopping centres: The case of Sonae Sierra. *International Journal of Retail and Distribution Management, 39*(6), 456–475. https://doi.org/10.1108/09590551111137994

Davidson, J. (2005). *Evaluation methodology basics: The nuts and bolts of sound evaluation.* SAGE Publications.

Food and Drug Administration. (2017). *Hazard analysis critical control point (HACCP) principles and application guidelines.* https://www.fda.gov/food/hazard-analysis-critical-control-point-haccp/haccp-principles-application-guidelines

Foster-Fishman, P., & Watson, E. (2011). The ABLe change framework: A conceptual and methodological tool for promoting systems change. *American Journal of Community Psychology, 49*(3–4), 503–516. https://doi.org/10.1007/s10464-011-9454-x

Frankhauser, P. (2015). From fractal urban pattern analysis to fractal urban planning concepts. In M. Helbich, J. Jokar Arsanjani, & M. Leitner (Eds.), *Computational approaches for urban environments. Geotechnologies and the environment* (Vol. 13; pp. 13–48). Springer. https://doi.org/10.1007/978-3-319-11469-9_2

Frederick, W. C. (1998). Creatures, corporations, communities, chaos, complexity: A naturological view of the corporate social role. *Business and Society, 37*(4), 358–376. https://doi.org/10.1177/000765039803700403

Friederici, P. (2009). *How a flock of birds can fly and move together.* Audubon. https://www.audubon.org/magazine/march-april-2009/how-flock-birds-can-fly-and-move-together

Friedman, M. (2005). *Trying hard is not good enough: How to produce measurable improvements for customers and communities.* Trafford.

Green, L. W., Kreuter, M. W., Deeds, S. G., Partridge, K. B., & Bartlett, E. (1980). *Health education planning: A diagnostic approach.* Mayfield Publishing.

Ison, R. L. (2008). Systems thinking and practice for action research. In P. W. Reason, & H. Bradbury (Eds.), *The SAGE handbook of action research participative inquiry and practice* (2nd ed.; pp. 139–158.). SAGE Publications.

Jackson, B. A., Faith, K. S., & Willis, H. H. (2012). Evaluating the reliability of emergency response systems for large-scale incident operations. *Rand Health Quarterly, 2*(3), 8.

Max, R. (2019). *Mall analytics.* Behavioral Analytics Retail. https://behavior analyticsretail.com/mall-analytics/

McGill, E., Marks, D., Er, V., Penney, T., Petticrew, M., & Egan, M. (2020). Qualitative process evaluation from a complex system perspective: A systematic review and framework for public health evaluators. *PLoS Med, 17*(11), e1003368. https://doi.org/10.1371/journal. pmed.1003368

Meadows, D. (2008). *Thinking in systems: A primer.* Chelsea Green Publishing.

Miller, J. G. (1978). *Living systems: The basic concepts.* https://www.panarchy. org/miller/livingsystems.html#Anchor-11-6296

NPR Staff. (2020, August 20). *How anchor stores keep neighborhoods afloat.* https://www.npr.org/2011/08/20/139815836/without-an-anchor -store-does-a-neighborhood-float-away

Renger, R., Foltysova, J., Renger, J., & Booze, W. (2017). Defining systems to evaluate system efficiency and effectiveness. *Evaluation Journal of Australasia, 17*(3), 4–13. https://doi.org/10.1177/1035719X1701700302

Renger, R., McPherson, M., Kontz-Bartels, T., & Becker, K. (2016). Process flow mapping for systems improvement: Lessons learned. *The Canadian Journal of Program Evaluation, 31*(1), 109–121.

TED. (2010, July 6). *Benoit Mandelbrot: Fractals and the art of roughness* [Video]. YouTube. https://www.youtube.com/watch?v=ay8OMOsf6AQ

Thomas, L. (2020, April 29). *Over 50% of department stores in malls predicted to close by 2021, real estate services firm says.* CNBC. https://www .cnbc.com/2020/04/29/50percent-of-all-these-malls-forecast-to -close-by-2021-green-street-advisors-says.html

Williams, B. (2014). *Week 36: Systems thinking.* Better Evaluation. https:// www.betterevaluation.org/en/blog/systems_thinking

Williams, B., & van 't Hof, S. (2016). *Wicked solutions: A systems approach to wicked problems* (2nd ed.). Bob Williams.

Principle. (2021, July 26). In Wikipedia. https://en.wikipedia.org/wiki/ Principle

Wolski, M. (2020). *System requirements—The context and boundary of a system.* https://michael.wolski.pro/2018/01/system-requirements-the-context -and-boundary-of-the-system/

World Health Organization. (2021, July 22). *Vaccine inequity undermining global economic recovery.* https://www.who.int/news/item/22-07 -2021-vaccine-inequity-undermining-global-economic-recovery

Yarbrough, D. B., Shula, L. M., Hopson, R. K., & Caruthers, F. A. (2010). *The program evaluation standards: A guide for evaluators and evaluation users* (3rd. ed). Corwin Press.

4

Cross-Cutting System Attributes

You're ready to evaluate a complex intervention acting as a system,
but is it ready for you?

Imagine that an agency approached you to complete an evaluation for them. You've gone through Meadow's (2008) questions and in conjunction with your understanding of system properties (Chapter 2), decided that what you are being asked to evaluate is a complex intervention acting as a system and not just a "bunch of stuff." Naturally, you decide that an evaluation approach aligned to the characteristics of the evaluand is appropriate: an approach grounded in an understanding of systems.

In my experience, the next challenge at this early stage of the evaluation is to determine whether the leadership, staff, and technology responsible for implementing the complex intervention are accepting and supportive of the evaluation. To answer this question, I conducted what I have coined a *system evaluation readiness scan* (SERS). The SERS involves assessing four system attributes: leadership, culture,

System Evaluation Theory, pages 55–78

information systems, and training. I refer to these as system attributes because they are qualities of a healthy system and necessary for an evaluation to be successful (Merriam-Webster, n.d.). I consider these attributes to be ubiquitous in that they are always influencing systems, at all system levels. In my experience, if any of these system attributes is missing, then there is a low probability the evaluation will be supported and/or the recommendations stemming from the evaluation will be used to make system improvements. You cannot assume these four attributes are present and operating. Further, you must consider the influence of these attributes throughout the course of the evaluation, but in particular at the bookends of the evaluation process.

I begin this chapter by explaining how the four attributes influence systems. I then revisit each attribute discussing how they might be assessed as part of the SERS. As you will learn, methods for evaluating these attributes from a systems perspective are in their infancy and as I write this it occurs to me that this may be a wonderful avenue for future evaluation research. Further, assuming methods for evaluating the attributes were available, it is my experience that you won't have the opportunity to evaluate them *before* you begin an evaluation. I can't imagine too many clients wanting to pay you just to decide whether they are ready to conduct an evaluation! Thus, for each attribute I offer some indicators that I have found helpful in assessing whether there will be support for the evaluation. It is my hope that by sharing these indicators with you it will stimulate you to think of other indicators and that in turn you will share these with our evaluation community. In Chapter 10, I revisit the four attributes and discuss how I use them at the back end of an evaluation to generate recommendations.

The Importance of the Four Attributes to Systems

Leadership

The importance of leadership to systems running efficiently and effectively is well documented in the organizational and business literature (Burke et al., 2006). However, with respect to systems there is an added dimension of leadership that must be considered: the ability to match one's thinking to the problem at hand, that is to use systems thinking to understand and solve system problems.

There is relatively little written with respect to the intersection between systems thinking and leadership. In one of the few studies, Southern (2020) noted that "systems leaders, [are] people who can create the conditions for collective creativity and collaborative action" (p. 2). I like this definition for two reasons. First, it directly ties the definitions of leadership and system together, highlighting the importance of the leader in creating the conditions necessary for interdependence and emergence. Second, it acknowledges that systems may have multiple leaders so as an evaluator you must be certain you include the perspectives of all key stakeholders (Heinz, 2019).

Leaders trained in systems thinking are also better able to identify a system, explain its properties, and the role of its parts (Reed, 2006). Further, leaders trained in systems thinking are adept at considering multiple perspectives thus enabling them to arrive at novel and innovative solutions to system problems; they are able to synthesize wisdom, creativity, and intelligences (Renger, 2021; Sternberg, 2007).

Senge et al. (2015) beautifully capture the importance of leaders' ability to consider multiple perspectives when problem solving in the following passage:

> Though they differ widely in personality and style, genuine system leaders have a remarkably similar impact. Over time, their profound commitment to the health of the whole radiates to nurture similar commitment in others.
>
> Their ability to see reality through the eyes of people very different from themselves encourages others to be more open as well. They build

relationships based on deep listening, and networks of trust and collaboration start to flourish.

They are so convinced that something can be done that they do not wait for a fully developed plan, thereby freeing others to step ahead and learn by doing.

Indeed, one of their greatest contributions can come from the strength of their ignorance, which gives them permission to ask obvious questions and to embody an openness and commitment to their own ongoing learning and growth that eventually infuse larger change efforts."

Building on the pioneering work of Chris Argyris, Tamarack (2020) notes that "out of the box" solutions require leaders to be double- and triple-loop learners.

Single-loop learning is about making adjustments to correct a mistake or a problem. It is focused on doing the things right. Causality might be observed but typically is not addressed.

Double-loop learning is identifying and understanding causality and then taking action to fix the problem. It is about doing the right things.

Triple-loop learning goes even deeper to explore our values and the reasons why we even have our systems, processes, and desired results in the first place. It is about trying to ascertain an understanding of how we make decisions that frame our work. (Tamarack, 2020, p. 1)

An excellent illustration of the difference between single, double, and triple loop learning occurred in my evaluation of a public health points of dispensing (POD) initiative. A POD is a complex intervention acting as a system whose purpose is to vaccinate as many people as possible, safely, in the shortest amount of time; that is to maximize throughput. I observed that incident commanders (the emergency response leaders), became fixated at the source of observed POD problems, like surges at the registration desk (Renger & Granillo, 2018). The incident commanders exhibited single-loop learning, trying to remedy the problem by relying on things they were trained to do, like increasing staffing or improving training at the site of the problem (Tamarack, 2020). They also limited the perspectives they were considering in solving the problem to those that were similarly trained: a kind of groupthink problem (Janis, 1991).

The actual POD surge was being caused by an upstream failure that created a cascading event. You will learn more about the cascading failure system principle in Chapter 7. By applying this system thinking principle I was able to determine that nonspecific public communication regarding vaccination scheduling was responsible for the surge: Everyone was showing up at the same time because the scheduling information was confusing. Had leadership been trained to consider the whole system they were observing, rather than one part of it, and consider different perspectives, that is, exhibit double- and triple-loop learning, then they would have been more likely to rapidly identify and resolve the problem.

At a higher system level, the COVID-19 pandemic provided a striking example of the impact a range of leadership involvement and styles can have on health, economic, and social systems. The contrasting leadership styles of Prime Minister Jacinda Arden, Chancellor Angela Merkel, and Presidents Jair Bolsonaro, Xi Jinping, and Donald Trump led to very different levels of system chaos with real world consequences (Kerrissey & Edmondson, 2020). Creating order, empathy, and authenticity are some leadership qualities essential to creating calm across the system so that it does not slip into chaos (Silard, 2020).

Information Systems

An information system (IS) is a "set of coordinated network components, which act together towards producing, distributing, and or processing information" ("Information Systems Versus Information Technology," n.d.).

I like this definition because it aligns nicely with our systems definition from Chapter 2, focusing on the coordination aspects of system components, or parts. The definition, however, might lead you to believe that systems thinking is inherent in IS design. But, as Atler (2004) noted, the IS field surprisingly lacks evidence of systems thinking. Thus, we cannot assume IS are inherently systemic in nature, reinforcing the need to define and evaluate IS underpinning the social systems they are intended to support.

A functional IS should support whatever the system actors (e.g., staff implementing the complex intervention) and other system parts (e.g., equipment) are trying to achieve; thereby contributing to the emergent system property. Because information systems mirror the complex interventions they are intended to support, I consider them a fractal and by definition a subsystem. For example, learning management system platforms are commonly used subsystems to support the delivery of complex educational interventions (Lewis et al., 2005). Learning management system platforms mirror the instructional processes they are intended to support. Similarly, web-emergency operation center (EOC) is an IS platform used in emergency management that mirrors the EOC incident command system (Johnson, 2012). Finally, there are numerous electronic healthcare record systems and health information exchange platforms that underlie complex health care systems. These platforms are critical for the system emergent property, continuity of care, to emerge (Jeddi et al., 2020; Kuperman, 2011).

One of the unique contributions of systems evaluation theory (SET) is its recognition of IS as a system attribute (Renger, 2015). There is no escaping the fact that IS has permeated every aspect of our life and has made us technology dependent. Anyone that has traveled can attest to the chaos that ensues when the travel reservation system "is down." Everything literally comes to standstill. The impact of IS has also been documented on health care, transportation, retail, and defense (Gunaskaran et al., 2006). If you doubt the dependence of any system on IS, then look no farther than the threat that cyber terrorism poses to our society and the crippling effects it can have (Furnell & Warren, 1999).

In my early publications I used the term *information technology* (IT) and not *information systems*. IT is a subset of information systems that focuses on computer use to achieve information management ("Information Systems Versus Information Technology," n.d). In other words, by using the term IT, I shifted the focus to just one part of the IS. In so doing, I neglected all the other necessary parts (people, processes, equipment) and their interdependencies, for information flow. What a mistake!

Culture

Culture refers to a large and diverse set of mostly intangible aspects of social life. According to sociologists, culture consists of the values, beliefs, systems of language, communication, and practices that people share in common and that can be used to define them as a collective (Cole, 2019).

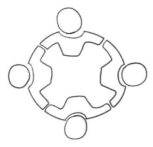

The influence of culture on systems is well documented (Parsons, 1972). Building on the work of Bronfenbrenner (1977), Vélez-Agosto et al. (2017) argue that "culture is not a separate system, but it is within everyday activities, routines, and practices" (p. 900). Indeed, how people think, their attitudes, and beliefs form the foundation of any system.

I find the iceberg metaphor from the Haines Institute useful in depicting the relationship between systems and culture. As you can see from Figure 4.1, culture is at the base of the iceberg, underscoring its importance in shaping system operations and behavior.

Another useful depiction of the importance of culture in systems is offered by Vélez-Agosto et al. (2017) who depict the omnipresent nature of culture as shown in Figure 4.2.

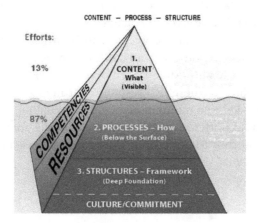

Figure 4.1 The Haines systems iceberg. *Source:* Used with permission and based on The Systems Thinking Approach® trademark registered and owned by the Haines Centre for Strategic Management Limited.

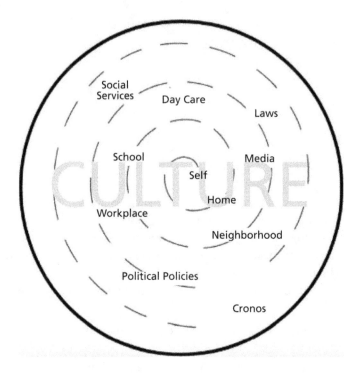

Figure 4.2 Depicting the centrality of culture in systems from Velez-Agosto et al. (2017).

In the pandemic, it was public health officials, not emergency managers, who took the lead role in the response. Remember, the response is a complex intervention acting as a system. In my evaluation I noted that one significant problem contributing to a disjointed and inefficient system response was a clash of cultures. Public health was concerned about health, while law enforcement was concerned about safety. The failure of these two response partners to create a shared understanding led to a monumental feud culminating in law enforcement's refusal to work with public health and doing an end-around by calling the governor to undermine public health mitigation strategies (Roorda et al., 2020).

Training

For a complex intervention acting as a system to operate efficiently and function effectively each part needs to complete its role when, where, and how it is required. Often system success hinges on human competencies and capabilities. Even in those cases where system processes are automated by IS, they must be first programmed by someone trained with the necessary IT and IS competencies and capabilities. The cross-cutting nature of competencies, and by extrapolation the training needed to develop those competencies, is illustrated in Haines' iceberg model (see Figure 4.1).

Training is designed to meet a need and an established standard (Fretwell et al., 2001). In Chapter 6, you will learn about how to operationalize the interdependence of system parts using process flow mapping to define system operating procedures (SOP). SOPs detail each process step, the sequence and timing in which they must be executed, and serve as the standard of acceptability against which to evaluate system interdependencies (Green et al., 1980). Therefore, system actors must be trained to ensure they are competent and capable of executing the SOPs.

The importance of a system actors' system thinking skills in influencing system efficiency is related to the level of system complexity. In less complex systems, there may be no need for the person executing a particular task to have an understanding of how the other parts work together. Thus, the training can be task-specific. For example, Henry Ford pioneered the assembly line, breaking the car assembly into 84 steps (Goss, 2020). Ford reasoned that assembly line workers didn't need to be experts in systems thinking; they didn't need to have an understanding of how the entire assembly line worked. This kept training costs low and it didn't take long to train a person with no previous skills to master any one of the 84 steps (A & E, 2020).

On the other hand, some systems, like the military, can benefit when people at the operational level are empowered to exercise their systems thinking skills. There are often unanticipated problems that require soldiers to be able to see the bigger picture and make decisions, that is "when in charge, take charge" (R. Hebb, personal communication,

January 15, 2021). Weick (2012) labeled this "emergent change" and described it as follows:

> Emergent change consists of ongoing accommodations, adaptations, and alterations that produce fundamental change without a priori intentions to do so. Emergent change occurs when people reaccomplish routines and when they deal with contingencies, breakdowns, and opportunities in everyday work. (p. 273)

When system actors operating at lower system levels are empowered and capable of solving problems without passing the problem up the chain, it can significantly improve system efficiency (L. Atkinson, personal communication, February 18, 2021).

In the pandemic, I observed innovative solutions to system problems coming from those working at an operational level who, because of their understanding of system interdependencies, developed efficient system bypasses. For example, county health officials recognized the delays being caused by relying on state level testing, and thus moved to a model of contracting with local laboratories to provide this service, cutting the wait time from 7–10 days down to 24–48 hours. At a lower operational level, systems thinkers in the EOC logistics section worked with IS to develop a way for businesses to make direct requests for PPE, rather than going through lengthy approval processes. These examples show how system actors with systems thinking skills at different system levels can improve system efficiency and effectiveness.

Research, however, on the utility of systems thinking training is mixed; individual behavior change seems to be possible, but the impact on organizational efficiency is less clear (Cavaleri & Sterman, 1998). My personal experience on the effectiveness of system thinking training echoes this observation. I have invested significant time in system thinking training for numerous graduate students. All of them seem to understand systems thinking at a theoretical level. However, only about half of them demonstrate the ability to apply what they learned! I recognize this could be a reflection of my teaching ability, the quality of opportunities structured for them to learn, innate ability, or motivation. Nevertheless, I wouldn't assume everyone who gets systems thinking training is willing or capable of applying systems thinking skills or indeed that the system in which they work is supportive of this type of thinking.

Evaluating the Attributes

I now discuss how the four attributes might be evaluated. The challenge, of course, in trying to assess the attributes *before* an evaluation, as part of your SERS, is that you likely don't have the access you need to the systems actors, source documentation, and so forth to make an assessment. Thus, I find myself relying on a "soft" set of indicators, borne out of an understanding of the research and my years of applied experience, or as Scott (2020) refers to it, my metis.[1] You may not agree with the indicators I use, but the point is that you must find some way, using your own indicators perhaps, to determine the likelihood the attributes needed for a successful evaluation are in place.

Leadership

System Thinking Skills

Currently, there are only a few tools available for evaluating the systems thinking skills of leaders. Adis et al. (2017) developed an extensive tool to assess eight systems thinking skills for leaders in the U.S. Army including cognitive flexibility, cognitive complexity, curiosity, pattern recognition, and openness to information. The Waters Foundation (2009) published a series of rubrics for evaluating systems thinking capabilities in persons of all ages. Some constructs include: (a) being able to change perspectives to increase understanding, (b) considering how mental models affect current reality, and (c) using understanding of system structure to identify possible leverage actions. I am still experimenting with the feasibility and utility of these instruments within different contexts. While I find it awkward to ask leaders to assess their own abilities, I find it a necessary avenue for exploration both for myself as an evaluator and for leaders personally as they become more self-aware through various reflective exercises.

A colleague, performer, sheep farmer, and close friend of mine Brian Keogh is exploring a promising avenue for evaluating leadership systems thinking skills called critical systems heuristics (Ulrich, 2018). Critical systems heuristics focuses on critical systems thinking, which is the ability to make judgments based on a consideration of system-wide perspectives. Ulrich's (2018) framework consists of 12 boundary categories grouped into four boundary issues (i.e., motivation, power, knowledge, and legitimation) that a leader uses to understand who is involved and who is affected by decisions in arriving at a rationale action for improving systems. I encourage you to commit to deepening your understanding of systems thinking leadership and what it might mean for you as part of your professional evaluation practice.

System Evaluation Readiness Scan Indicators

Evaluating a complex intervention acting as a system is not difficult, but it does take time, resources, and commitment. Leadership is critical for getting cooperation from all the system parts at all system levels and to leverage the resources needed to see the evaluation through from start to finish (Hitt & Duane, 2002; Patton, 2008).

I use the following indicators as red flags for leadership's lack of motivation and buy-in to the evaluation:

- primary purpose of the evaluation is to check off a funding requirement;
- suggestion that the evaluation is needed to prove something they already know;
- lack of timely response to evaluation requests;
- poor quality feedback (e.g., nonspecific, delayed, irrelevant);

- no access or interaction given to other decision-makers or system actors; and
- no investment or in-kind contributions to the evaluation (Becker et al., 2015).

When the motivation for my services is to just meet a funding requirement, I worry the evaluation is what I call a "checkbox exercise." When the client is searching for evidence to justify what they are already doing and the way they do it, then I worry there will be a strong flavor of confirmation bias to the evaluation. The presence of some or all these indicators suggests that leadership isn't necessarily invested in the evaluation and if one is conducted, then little or no change will occur, and the evaluation will likely be shelved (Friedman, 2009).

In my experience, when any of these indicators are present, there will be little, if any, support for the evaluation. In fact, when these indicators are present, they are often accompanied by efforts to bias, or even undermine, the evaluation. I usually refuse to conduct evaluations when any of these red flag indicators are present. However, I understand the willingness to turn down work depends on your career and economic circumstances. I'm not naïve; sometimes you need the work to put food on the table. However, before you jump in feet first to conduct an evaluation that is not being supported by leadership consider the impact on your reputation and likelihood of securing future work too!

_____

Information Systems

Information Systems Functionality

There are measures of IS functionality, such as the Software Usability Measurement Inventory questionnaire, which measures five quality components of IS systems: affect, efficiency, helpfulness, control, and learnability (Jeddi et al., 2020). Of particular interest to SET are the efficiency and learnability components. Efficiency is defined as "the relation between (a) the accuracy and completeness with which users achieve certain goals and (b) the resources expended in achieving them" (Jeddi et al., 2020, p. 2). The efficiency component as defined by Jeddi et al. (2020) could be used to supplement SET measures of efficiency (Chapter 7). The learnability component is defined as "the speed and facility with which the user feels that they have been able to master the system, or to learn how to use new features when necessary" (Jeddi et al., 2020, p. 2). This definition provides additional perspective as to how one might operationalize and evaluate the training needed for system actors.

I anchor my evaluation of IS to the following three goals:

■ to produce,
■ process, and
■ distribute information.

To evaluate these IS goals I tend to prefer to speak with system actors at the operational level, rather than leadership. It is my experience that those who depend on IS to complete operational aspects of the complex intervention acting as a system are best able to comment on its ability to meet the three goals.

System Evaluation Readiness Scan Indicators

I do my best to listen for key words and phrases used by system actors that provide insight into whether the IS goals are being met and/or I can count on the IS to support the evaluation. Some examples from my evaluations include: "The computer is down again"; "My email keeps disappearing"; "I can't find the [data] field I need"; "The system is so slow today [actually all the time]"; "My computer always freezes"; "They [the company] won't buy us the computers we need to do our job"; "We are using an outdated version of Windows"; and so on. As I noted above, I try not to fixate on a single indicator and instead practice active listening (Ison, 2008), honing in on any clues that the IS system is or is not working as it should.

Of course, with any IS problem you must balance whether it is an IS or user issue (Rose, 2003). Therefore, it is important to gather the perspectives of as many system actors as possible, assuming of course, that leadership provides such access (see below).

Culture

Shared Culture

Cole (2019) notes the intangibility of culture is what makes it so challenging to evaluate. One way to operationalize culture for evaluation purposes comes from Heinz (2009) who notes that shared values are a key component to successful organizational cultures. For evaluation purposes, I operationalize shared values as a common understanding of the emergent system property. Thus, it is important to evaluate the extent to which system actors have a shared understanding of the emergent system property. I usually do this qualitatively, by facilitating group meetings between leadership and system actors representing the different system parts.

System Evaluation Readiness Scan Indicators

There are four questions, the answers to which, provide an indication as to whether the culture is conducive to an evaluation:

- "Can I get access to talk to some of the system actors?"
- "Are staff permitted to speak freely in meetings with leadership present?" (Detert, 2003)
- "Can I get access to source documents?"
- "Are SOPs in place?"

When leaders help facilitate the access to actors at the operational level, I feel confident that transparency is valued. Transparency is critical to the success of an evaluation. Another dimension of transparency is the ability of staff members to speak freely. I'm sure many of you can resonate with being in a meeting where there is an awkward silence among staff as leadership explains what they believe to be the state of affairs that does not coincide with reality. As you learned in Chapter 1, one of the tenets of systems thinking is perspectives. It is impossible to gather perspectives to round out your picture of the puzzle if system actors are not allowed to, or do not feel they can, speak freely.

Access to source documents, such as mission statements, meeting minutes, and SOPs serve two purposes (Renger, 2011). First, when they are provided, it further reinforces that I am working with a system that values transparency. Second, the source documents, like SOPs, let me know that the organization values documentation, which is critical for the success of a system and the evaluation. For example, the presence of workflows, another name for SOPs, in medical systems indicates to me that the system is advanced and that leadership and system actors understand that system training and improvements are contingent upon making explicit how the system is supposed to work.

Some other indicators I use to evaluate the system culture include:

- staff turnover rate
- organizational structure

The greater the staff turnover, generally the less stable the system. Stability of system actors, especially system leaders, is important for the success of an evaluation. Without stability in the system, evaluations often need to be revamped to meet the mandate of the new leaders. This can also mean that ongoing evaluations get discarded and related resources are never used to help make decisions.

> Throughout my career, I worked on numerous lengthy evaluation projects spanning multiple leadership changes. Within these projects I found myself essentially being the organizational memory. This is an enormous responsibility and one with many ethical challenges, especially being an external evaluator sometimes holding more knowledge of the system than the actors within. I believe our field would benefit greatly into research expounding upon and carefully delineating the evaluator's responsibilities under these circumstances.

With respect to organizational structure, much can be learned from an organizational chart. The more hierarchical the system structure, the more rigid it will be (Heinz, 2019). Leaders in these structures often are not system thinkers and they don't take into consideration other perspectives when trying to troubleshoot. They are also slow to act on evaluation recommendations. On the other end of the spectrum are clan cultures, who have a flat organizational chart to encourage collaboration and teamwork (Heinz, 2019). Clan cultures in my experience, are the most receptive and responsive to a systems evaluation.

Training

System Actor Competence and Capabilities to Execute System Processes

Although evaluating whether system actors have the necessary training to execute SOPs is conceptually straightforward, it should not be taken for granted. For example, in Chapter 3 you learned about simple, ordering generating rules that can help explain why complex interventions acting as systems are organized the way they are (Burnes, 2005). Simple, order generating rules describe a process that must be executed. In nature, the rules underlying a system process occur automatically (Stacey, 2003). However, as both Stacey (2003) and Burnes (2005) point out, human beings have a free will and can interpret such rules in "widely different ways" (Burnes, 2005, p. 83). Thus, for a system to operate efficiently and as intended it is important to ensure that all system actors are trained in even what may appear to be the simplest of processes.

There is a plethora of research and models dedicated to evaluating training, such as Kirkpatrick and Kirkpatrick's four levels: learner satisfaction, learner competency, learner behavior, and organizational benefits (Kirkpatrick & Kirkpatrick, 2006; Mohammed Saad & Mat, 2013). In practice, however, it is unlikely leadership will be willing to invest the time and resources to evaluate staff competencies and capabilities. After all, they selected staff through a recruitment process (internal or external) that presumably rests on demonstrating competency and capability. Therefore, I often engage in more of a checklist exercise to verify whether the staff have the necessary credentials and certifications (Gawande, 2009). This has proven a fast and effective way to identify macro training issues. For example, in the pandemic response I learned that many public health trained staff were assigned to incident command roles for which they were unacceptably underqualified. In my evaluation report I emphasized that a department administrator does not necessarily make a good incident commander.

System Evaluation Readiness Scan Indicators

For the evaluation to be successful I need to work with people who understand the system (i.e., complex intervention). Degrees and certifications are important in evaluating training, but the reality is that only 27%

of college graduates work in the field in which they were trained (Coffee et al., 2019). By extrapolation then, many of the system actors you encounter will likely have received some form of "on-the-job training." Two of the most important predictors of success of on-the-job training are self-efficacy and prior experience with tasks (van der Klink & Streumer, 2002). Therefore, two of the most important SERS training indicators I use are:

■ Tenure
■ System progression

System actors that have come up through the system, that is promoted from within, are likely to have a good understanding of the system functioning. Their promotion also indicates that they have demonstrated competency/capability and are valued by system leadership. System actors with long tenure and evidence of promotion, (i.e., coming from a "grow-your-own" system culture), will have unique perspectives of different parts of the complex intervention acting as a system, especially the interdependence of system parts. Such actors are key for being able to define how the system works; a key first step in evaluating complex interventions operating and functioning as a system.

The Interdependence of System Attributes

There is considerable research evidence to support the interdependence between leadership, IT, training, and culture. For example, effective leaders are those who have been trained to be systems thinkers (Bleich, 2014a, 2014b), leaders are responsible for instilling the culture necessary for system change (Gill, 2002; Ionescu, 2014; Slavin et al., 2012), and culture is a key influence on the adoption of IT (Leidner & Kayworth, 2006).

Parsons (1972) argued that culture itself is a system "which is specifically concerned with systems of meaning" (p. 256) and social systems are the link to providing this meaning. He goes on to say that culture is "essentially the desirable pattern of interactions and these patterns are the standards by which unit action shall be evaluated" (p. 257). Parson's work is heavily theoretical and difficult to digest, but I interpreted his arguments to suggest that culture is what emerges when the system parts interact as they are intended. So, for example, one might argue that Henry Ford structured his system to maximize productivity by minimizing the level of cooperation (i.e., manipulating the culture) needed between workers on the assembly line. On the other hand, the

COVID-19 response is optimized by maximizing a culture of cooperation and coordination between system elements.

Thus, it may be that system interdependencies give rise to at least
two emergent properties. The first, as you learned in Chapter 2, is the
essential system property. The second is the system culture. It is my contention that these two emergent system properties are themselves interdependent. For example, the pandemic response system consisted of
many interdependent agencies whose ability to save lives depended on
the emergence of a culture of cooperation and coordination. While initially I thought the emergent nature of culture to be a unique thought,
as with many of my thoughts I have come to realize that it is not novel
at all and has been pondered and debated by other scholars who note
that culture emerges from the actions of human beings in certain contexts (Vélez-Agosto et al., 2017).

In my early publications I treated the four system attributes as independent influences, each important in their own right in influencing
the efficiency and effectiveness of complex interventions operating
and functioning as systems, respectively. My work since then has
validated the importance of considering these attributes through the
lifetime of a systems evaluation. However, as my own systems thinking skills have evolved and I've consciously practiced systems thinking (Ison, 2008), I have come to see these factors not as independent
influences, but themselves as interdependent parts.

Conclusion

In this chapter you learned about four system attributes that bookend
the systems evaluation approach. This chapter focused on using these
attributes to help assess whether the ground is fertile for an evaluation.
Of the four system attributes, leadership is by far the most important
in ensuring a successful evaluation. If leadership is not on board, then
there is a good chance you will be swimming upstream the entire course
of the evaluation and the evaluation results will be meaningless and/or
shelved. In Chapter 6 I provide examples of how to engage leadership
from the onset and to continually engage them in the evaluation process.

In Chapter 10 I discuss how these four system attributes are also
the basis for making recommendations. When system processes break
down it's often because leadership wasn't engaged, system actors lacked

training to execute systems processes, information systems failed, and/ or a culture of cooperation and coordination was missing.

Note

1. "We can find in the Greek concept of metis a means of comparing the forms of knowledge embedded in local experience with the more general, abstract knowledge deployed by the state and its technical agencies" (Scott, 2020, p. 311).

References

A & E. (2020). *America the story of us.* History Channel. https://www.history.com/shows/america-the-story-of-us

Adis, C., Wisecarver, M., Raber, C., Wind, A. P., & Canali, K. G. (2017). *Innovative tools to assess systems thinking ability* (Technical Report 1362). United States Army Research Institute for the Behavioral and Social Sciences. https://apps.dtic.mil/sti/pdfs/AD1045468.pdf

Atler, S. (2004). *Desperately seeking systems thinking in the information systems discipline.* ICIS 2004 proceedings. https://aisel.aisnet.org/icis 2004/61

Becker, K., Renger, R., & McPherson, M. (2015). Indicators of buy-in to gauge evaluation success. *Evaluation Journal of Australasia, 15*(2), 12–21. https://doi.org/10.1177/1035719X1501500203

Bleich, M. R. (2014a). Developing leaders as system thinkers—Part III. *The Journal of Continuing Education in Nursing, 45*(6), 246–248. http://doi.org/10.3928/00220124-20140527-12

Bleich, M. R. (2014b). Developing leaders as system thinkers—Part I. *The Journal of Continuing Education in Nursing, 45*(4), 158–159. http://doi.org/10.3928/00220124-20140327-13

Burke, C. S., Stagl, K. C., Klein, C., Goodwin, G. F., Salas, E., & Halpin, S. M. (2006). What type of leadership behaviors are functional in team? A meta-analysis. *The Leadership Quarterly, 17*(3), 288–307. https://doi.org/10.1016/j.leaqua.2006.02.007

Burnes, B. (2005). Complexity theory and organizational change. *International Journal of Management Reviews, 7*(2), 73–90. https://doi.org/10.1111/j.1468-2370.2005.00107.x

Bronfenbrenner, U. (1977). Toward an experimental ecology of human development. *American Psychologist, 32*(7), 513–531. https://doi.org/10.1037/0003-066X.32.7.513

Cavaleri, S., & Sterman, J. D. (1998). Towards evaluation of systems-thinking interventions: A case study. *System Dynamics Review: The Journal of the System Dynamics Society, 13*(2), 171–186. https://onlinelibrary.wiley.

com/doi/abs/10.1002/(SICI)1099-1727(199722)13:2<171::AID
-SDR123>3.0.CO;2-9

Coffee, C., Sentz, R., & Saleh, Y. (2019, August). *Degrees at work: Examining the serendipitous outcomes of diverse degrees.* Emsi. https://www.economic modeling.com/degrees-at-work/

Cole, N. L. (2019). *So what is culture, exactly?* Thought Co. https://www .thoughtco.com/culture-definition-4135409

Detert, J. R. (2003). *To speak or not to speak: Multi-level leadership influences on organizational voice.* Doctoral thesis. Harvard University, Cambridge, Mass. (May).

Fretwell, D. H., Lewis, M. V., & Deij. A. (2001). *A framework for defining and assessing occupational standards in developing countries.* World Bank, Human Development Network, ERIC Clearinghouse on Adult, Career, and Vocational Education. https://www.researchgate.net/ publication/237431623

Friedman, M. (2009). *Video introduction to result based accountability* [Video]. YouTube. https://youtu.be/RtBC89F3Xi4

Furnell, S. M., & Warren, M. J. (1999). Computer hacking and cyber terrorism: The real threats in the new millennium. *Computers and Security, 18*(1), 28–34. https://doi.org/10.1016/S0167-4048(99)80006-6

Gawande, A. (2009). *The checklist manifesto: How to get things right.* Metropolitan Books.

Gill, R. (2002). Change management—or change leadership? *Journal of Change Management, 3*(4), 307–318. https://doi.org/10.1080/71402 3845

Goss, J. L. (2020). *Henry Ford and the auto assembly line.* Thought Co. https:// www.thoughtco.com/henry-ford-and-the-assembly-line-1779201

Green, L. W., Kreuter, M. W., Deeds, S. G., Partridge, K. B., & Bartlett, E. (1980). *Health education planning: A diagnostic approach.* Mayfield Publishing.

Gunasekaran, A., Ngai, E. W. T., & McGaughey, R. E. (2006). Information technology and systems justification: A review for research and applications. *European Journal of Operational Research, 173*(3), 957–983. https://doi.org/10.1016/j.ejor.2005.06.002

Heinz, K. (2019). *The four types of organizational culture you should know.* Built In. https://builtin.com/company-culture/types-of-organizational -culture

Hitt, M. A., & Duane, R. (2002). The essence of strategic leadership: Managing human and social capital. *Journal of Leadership & Organizational Studies, 9*(1), 3–14. https://doi.org/10.1177/107179190200900101

Information Systems Versus Information Technology. (n.d.). *Management study guide.* https://www.managementstudyguide.com/information -system-and-information-technology.htm

Ionescu, V. C. (2014). Leadership, culture and organizational change. *Manager, 20*(1), 65–71.

Ison, R. L. (2008). Systems thinking and practice for action research. In P. W. Reason & H. Bradbury (Eds.), *The SAGE handbook of action research participative inquiry and practice* (2nd ed.; pp. 139–158.). SAGE Publications.

Janis, I. (1991). Groupthink. In E. Griffin (Ed.), *A first look at communication theory* (pp. 235–246). McGraw Hill.

Jeddi, F. R., Nabovati, E., Bigham, R., & Khajouei, R. (2020). Usability evaluation of a comprehensive national health information system: Relationship of quality components to users' characteristics. *International Journal of Medical Informatics, 133*, 104026. https://doi.org/10.1016/j.ijmedinf.2019.104026

Johnson, T. (2012). Emergency management students' perceptions of the use of WEBEOC to support authentic learning. *Educational Media International, 49*(3), 171–182. https://doi.org/10.1080/09523987.2012.738010

Kerrissey, M. J., & Edmondson, A. C. (2020). What good leadership looks like in this pandemic. *Harvard Business Review.* https://hbr.org/2020/04/what-good-leadership-looks-like-during-this-pandemic

Kirkpatrick, D. L., & Kirkpatrick, J. D. (2006). *Evaluating training programs: The four levels.* Berrett-Koehler.

Kuperman, G. J. (2011). Health-information exchange: Why are we doing it, and what are we doing? *Journal of the American Medical Informatics Association, 18*(5), 678–682. https://doi.org/10.1136/amiajnl-2010-000021

Leidner. D. E., & Kayworth, T. (2006). Review: A review of culture in information systems research: Toward a theory of information technology culture conflict. *MIS Quarterly, 30*(2), 357–399. https://www.jstor.org/stable/25148735

Lewis, B. A., MacEntee, V. M., DeLaCruz, S., Englander, C., Jeffery, T., Takach, E., Wilson, S., & Wodall, J. (2005, June 16–19). *Learning management system comparisons.* Proceedings of the 2005 Informing Science and IT Education Joint Conference. Flagstaff, AZ.

Meadows, D. (2008). *Thinking in systems: A primer.* Chelsea Green Publishing.

Merriam-Webster. (n.d.). Attribute. https://www.merriam-webster.com/dictionary/attribute

Mohammed Saad, A., & Mat, N. (2013). Evaluation of effectiveness of training and development: The Kirkpatrick model. *Asian Journal of Business and Management Sciences, 2*(11), 14–24. https://repo.uum.edu.my/id/eprint/9415

Parsons, T. (1972). Culture and social systems revisited. *Social Science Quarterly, 53*(2), 253–266. http://www.jstor.org/stable/42858956

Patton, M. Q. (2008). *Utilization-focused evaluation.* SAGE Publications. https://doi.org/10.1177/1098214010373646

Reed, G. E. (2006). Leadership and systems thinking. *Defense AT&L, 35*(3), 10–13.

Renger, R. (2011). Constructing and verifying program theory using source documentation. *The Canadian Journal of Program Evaluation, 25*(1), 51–67.

Renger, R. (2015). System evaluation theory (SET). *Evaluation Journal of Australasia, 15*(4), 16–28. https://doi.org/10.1177/1035719X150150 0403

Renger, R. (2021). COVID-19: Exposing the need for emergency management to invest in systems thinking. *Journal of Emergency Management, 19*(7), 39–48. https://doi.org/10.5055/jem.0607

Renger, R., & Granillo, B. (2018). Using systems evaluation theory (SET) to improve points of dispensing (POD) planning, training, and evaluation. *Journal of Emergency Management, 16*(3), 149–157. https://doi .org/10.5055/jem.2018.0364

Roorda, M., Gullickson, A., & Renger, R. (2020). Whose values? Decision-making in a COVID-19 emergency-management situation. *Evaluation Matters—He Take Tō Te Aromatawai, 6.* https://doi.org/10.18296/em .0057

Rose, E. (2003). *User error: Resisting computer culture.* Between the Lines.

Scott, J. (2020). Thin simplifications and practical knowledge: Metis. In, *Seeing like a state* (pp. 309–341). Yale University Press. https://doi .org/10.12987/9780300252989-011

Senge, P., Hamilton, H., & Kania, J. (2015). The dawn of system leadership. *Stanford Social Innovation Review, 13*(1), 27–33.

Silard, A. (2020). 3 strategies for effective leadership during the pandemic: Understand the unique abilities of required of leaders during a crisis like COVID. *Psychology Today.* https://www.psychologytoday .com/us/blog/the-art-living-free/202006/3-strategies-effective -leadership-during-the-pandemic

Slavin, S. J., Schindler, D., Chibnall, J. T., Fendell, G., & Shoss, M. (2012). PERMA: A model for institutional leadership and culture change. *Academic Medicine, 87*(11), 1481. https://doi.org/10.1097/ACM .0b013e31826c525a

Southern, N. (2020). Creating leaders for systems complexity. In G. Metcalf, K. Kijima, H. Deguchi (Eds.), *Handbook of systems sciences.* Springer. https://doi.org/10.1007/978-981-13-0370-8_15-1

Stacey, R. D. (2003). *Strategic management and organisational dynamics: The challenge of complexity.* Prentice Hall.

Sternberg, R. J. (2007). A systems model of leadership: WICS. *American Psychologist, 62*(1), 34–42. https://doi.org/10.1037/0003-066X.62.1.34

Tamarack. (2020). *Tool: Single, double, and triple loop learning.* https:// www.tamarackcommunity.ca/library/single-double-and-triple-loop -learning-tool

Ulrich, W. (2018). *A mini-primer for critical systems heuristics (CSH).* https:// wulrich.com/csh.html van der Klink, M. R., & Streumer, J. N. (2002). Effectiveness of on-the-job training. *Journal of European Industrial Training, 26*(2), 196–199. https://doi.org/10.1108/03090590210422076

Vélez-Agosto, N. M., Soto-Crespo, J. G., Vizcarrondo-Oppenheimer, M., Vega-Molina, S., & Coll, C. G. (2017). Bronfenbrenner's bioecological theory revision: Moving culture from the macro into the micro. *Perspectives on Psychological Science, 12*(5), 900–910. https://doi.org/10.1177/1745691617704397

Waters Foundation. (2009). *Systems thinking rubrics: Systems thinking in schools.* https://waterscenterst.org/

Weick, K. E. (2012). *Making sense of the organization, Volume 2: The impermanent organization* (Vol. 2). John Wiley & Sons.

5

The Why Behind System Evaluation Theory

To problem solve you need to know the why behind the how.

This chapter tells my personal story of the why behind the how of how systems evaluation theory ([SET]; Renger, 2015) came to be.

Let's assume at this point in your system's journey you have decided that the complex intervention you are evaluating is operating and functioning as a system. You also have confidence through your systems evaluation readiness scan that there is support to complete a systems evaluation. So now it's time to plan the evaluation. McGill et al. (2020) stated that from a "systems perspective, the role of the evaluator is to make sense of the interplay between the complex system and the (simple or complex) intervention to help explain health and other impacts and inform future decisions about implementation." (p. 4). SET helps evaluators fulfill this role by providing them with the blueprint to complete a systems evaluation.

System Evaluation Theory, pages 79–96
Copyright © 2022 by Information Age Publishing
www.infoagepub.com

A theory to guide the evaluation per se should not be confused with other theories, like program and social science theories. In Figure 5.1 you can see that there are many social science branches. Each branch generates theories; ideas how the world works. Some of these theories, or combination of them, can form the basis for a program or policy. That basis or underlying assumptions upon which the program is predicated is called the program theory (Chapter 1).

The need for a program theory in evaluation is guided by a particular theoretical approach called methods-based evaluation (Christie

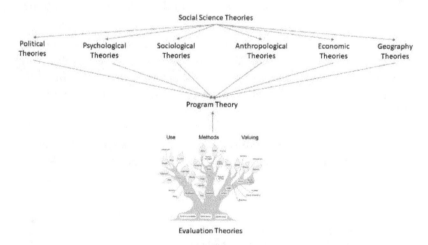

Figure 5.1 The relationship between different theory types. SET is an evaluation theory that embraces the evaluation theories of use, methods, and valuing.

& Alkin, 2013). However, a program evaluation could be guided by evaluation theories grounded in use or valuing or some combination of all three.

Based on a review of 21 evaluation studies evaluating systems McGill et al. (2020) concluded that the underlying theory guiding an evaluation is often unclear. SET is an evaluation theory that uses a combination of use, methods, and value evaluation theories to evaluate a complex intervention. SET guides the evaluator through three steps: defining the complex intervention acting as a system, evaluating its efficiency (i.e., system interdependencies), and evaluating its effectiveness (i.e., system emergence). As you learned in Chapter 1, understanding the why is helpful in orienting your decision-making (Sinek, 2009; Sweet, 2017). Despite best intentions there always seems to be something that doesn't quite go according to plan in any evaluation. The only way to make meaningful corrections to your systems evaluation plan is to understand the rationale behind the structure and sequencing of SET's three steps. This chapter is devoted to providing you that rationale, starting with the telling of a story about what led me to developing SET.

How It Started

In 2013 I left my 18-year position at the University of Arizona to accept a position at the University of North Dakota to help establish a new Master of Public Health program with an evaluation specialty. About 3 months into the new position, I received a call from my department's deputy director asking whether I could meet with Tom Nehring, the North Dakota state emergency medical services (EMS) director, to help with an evaluation project.

In a 90-minute call that began late in the afternoon, Tom explained that the state of North Dakota had just received a sizable grant from the Leona M., & Harry B. Helmsley Charitable Trust (hereinafter referred to as Helmsley) to distribute and train EMS personnel across the state in using the LUCAS2™ device (Figure 5.2). I explained to Tom that I had no substantive EMS expertise and asked him to explain the device's purpose. Tom explained the LUCAS2 was intended to save the lives of those experiencing a sudden cardiac arrest (SCA). During a SCA the heart stops beating and the blood flow to the brain stops. Blood flow must be restored within 4–6 minutes and advanced life support within 12 minutes to prevent permanent brain damage and to save lives (Cummins et al., 1985).

Figure 5.2 The LUCAS2™ device (Physio-Control Lucas 2 Chest Compression System - 99576-000011 - Recertified | MME [mmemed.com]).

Cardiopulmonary resuscitation (CPR) is a way of manually forcing blood flow during a SCA. High-quality CPR (i.e., that is performed with the required compression rate, depth, and fraction), is proven to save lives (Yannopoulos, 2015). However, delivering high-quality CPR is difficult for even the most highly trained emergency medical technicians (EMTs). Administering high-quality CPR is physically exhausting and difficult to sustain for even just a few minutes (Yang et al., 2013).

In a rural setting, maintaining high-quality CPR is especially challenging because EMS transport time can often exceed 30 minutes. When possible, EMTs take turns delivering CPR, but even the smallest interruptions, or pauses, in CPR adversely influence patient outcomes (Olasveengen et al., 2009). To further complicate matters, often rural EMS services only consist of two volunteer EMTs: one driver and one in the back attending to the patient. Thus, the onus of providing high-quality CPR over an extended period often falls on a single EMT. In short, these factors make the likelihood of surviving a SCA in rural America bleak.

Tom further explained that the LUCAS2 was a battery-operated device designed to address the challenge of delivering continuous, high-quality CPR by providing automatic mechanical chest compressions. Tom wanted to know whether I could evaluate the success of the LUCAS2 device in improving patient outcomes. He said he needed a proposal by the next morning!

As I worked on the proposal through the night, I wondered how I could isolate the effect of the LUCAS2 or how I might be able to determine what proportion of saved lives could be attributed to the device. Upon reflection, I was paralyzed by my training in reductionist thinking, focusing on whether it was possible to isolate the cause and effect of the LUCAS2.

In my proposal to Tom, I reiterated my lack of substantive EMS expertise and indicated that I didn't think it would be possible to ever say definitively whether the LUCAS2 device was responsible for a better patient outcome. In describing the evaluation challenge, I wrote that "the LUCAS2 seemed to be one of many moving parts in the cardiac system of care." I further explained that because there were so many interacting variables (i.e., puzzle pieces), isolating the effect of the LUCAS2 using traditional research designs, like a randomized control trial (Chapter 1) would require numerous control groups. This, together with the fact that SCA is a relatively rare event, would mean such a study would need to go on for years, if not decades to achieve the necessary statistical power. Further, such a study, if feasible, would have serious challenges getting past an ethics review committee; you simply couldn't randomize people such that some would not have access to the life-saving technology.

Tom called the next morning. I was surprised by the excitement in his voice, after all the proposal was poorly written and offered no real way forward vis à vis the evaluation. Tom had picked up on my inadvertent use of the phrase "cardiac care system" and asked whether an evaluation of the entire cardiac care system was possible. I told him to my knowledge no one had ever evaluated an entire system and I assumed to do so would be costly. Tom then mentioned that his grant was part of a seven-state grant (Figure 5.3). He asked me whether the

Figure 5.3 The seven states of cardiac systems of care evaluation (Booze & Weinkauf, 2013).

evaluation of the cardiac system of care would be possible if the evaluation line items from the seven grants were combined.

Soon after I was sitting in Sioux Falls, South Dakota meeting with a Helmsley project officer. I stated my interest in pursuing the evaluation of the cardiac care system, but confessed that I did not know exactly how to proceed because to my knowledge there was no evaluation theory for evaluating complex interventions operating and functioning as systems. The project officer understood this barrier, but placed confidence in me to develop a solution. I left that meeting with a $4 million dollar evaluation budget for evaluating cardiac care systems in seven states with no specific deliverable! To this day I cannot believe my good fortune and I am forever indebted to Helmsley for a once in a lifetime opportunity. I vowed I would do everything in my power to use that opportunity to advance our discipline's ability to evaluate systems. My systems journey had begun in earnest.

An important takeaway from this experience is that honesty really is the best policy. By admitting I didn't know the path forward it created trust in my client and funder to provide that opportunity for me. As you will learn in the book's final chapter, the perceived elitism of evaluators is a significant deterrent in clients working with us and attracting new talent to our discipline.

Building My Systems Thinking Competencies and Capabilities

My quest for an understanding of systems began by reading the work of von Bertalanffy, who some consider the father of modern-day general systems theory (von Bertalanffy, 1972). To better understand general systems theory, I hired a biologist to teach me system basics. As I learned about a particular system principle, I looked for instances where it might be operating in the cardiac care system. For example, after learning about the feedback loop principle I began looking for places in the cardiac care system where information was being exchanged, like between EMTs, between dispatch and the EMS service, between the EMS and the hospital, and so forth. What I discovered is there were literally hundreds of places in the cardiac system of care that depended on feedback loops! This began opening my eyes to the power of systems thinking and systems principles.

Although some have labeled von Bertalanffy as the "father" of systems thinking, systems thinking is central to and permeates Indigenous cultures, suggesting that the "mother" of systems thinking far predates the work of von Bertalanffy (Yunkaporta, 2020).

One example of a feedback loop pertains to the run-report data collected by EMTs. A run report specifies the details of the EMS response (e.g., patient vitals, response time, etc.) and is completed after the EMT's drop off their patient at a hospital. Run reports are then uploaded by EMS services to the state, who in turn merge the run-report data with hospital data to better understand the relationship between care provided on scene and the patient outcomes. In this way, ambulatory care and tertiary care data are used together to help inform decision-making.

I discovered many states were not sharing the results of the uploaded run reports with their EMS services in a timely manner. Further, when feedback was provided it often lacked relevance and specificity to guide EMS services in making appropriate corrective actions to improve their SCA response. This lack of feedback negatively impacted EMTs' motivation for completing run reports. As a result, the run reports were often uploaded late and/or were incomplete. This was a negative feedback cycle spiraling out of control.

It occurred to me certain criteria needed to be met for feedback loops to be effective. I researched the continuous quality improvement literature and identified five key criteria for effective feedback (Agency for Healthcare Research and Quality, 2021; Mcshane & Von Glinow, 2009). You will learn about these feedback criteria, plus one I added, in Chapter 7. I then applied these criteria to evaluate each feedback loop I identified. By applying these criteria, I was able to recommend that states begin providing regular monthly feedback pertaining to the run reports back to the EMS services. Within 3 months, run-report compliance and quality (as judged by the number of complete reports submitted on time), for one state had increased 30%.

After 17 years of writing recommendations for program evaluations that, in all honesty, mostly went unheeded, I can't express in words how rewarding and motivating it was to see my evaluation recommendation immediately implemented and making a positive difference. Reflecting on that experience, it was the first time I engaged in and applied systems thinking: I had taken a system principle (i.e., feedback loop), used it to identify a type of interdependence between system parts, added an evaluator's understanding of need for a standard of acceptability against which to make judgements, and, voila! I was providing system users with meaningful improvement recommendations (Checkland, 2000).

I continued the same learning pattern, whereby I would be introduced to a new system principle, identify where that principle might be operating in the cardiac care system, and apply it to make recommendations for system improvement. After about a year I realized I needed to be more methodical in how I applied systems principles to evaluating a system. I needed an evaluation theory to guide the practice of evaluating systems.

Formulating System Evaluation Theory

Alkin (1969) wrote that a theory of evaluation should: (a) offer a conceptual scheme by which evaluation areas or problems are classified, (b) provide systems of generalizations about the use of various evaluation procedures and techniques and their appropriateness to evaluation areas or problems, and (c) define the strategies including kinds of data, and means of analysis and reporting appropriate to each of the areas of the conceptual scheme. I now discuss how SET meets each of Alkin's criteria, albeit not in the same order.

1. Meeting Alkin's First Criterion: Systems Evaluation Theory's Conceptual Scheme

I began by searching the literature for conceptual schemes for evaluating complex interventions acting as systems. There were many theories to guide evaluating programs (Mertens & Wilson, 2019), but relatively little for evaluating complex interventions acting as systems. One promising publication was that by Cabrera and Trochim (2006) entitled "A Theory of Systems Evaluation" (TES). TES was good in that it encouraged me to think more deliberately about using systems thinking to understand how to tailor an evaluation fit for purpose (Williams, 2010). However, as Cabrera and Trochim (2006) wrote, "Of course, all theories and models are eventually wrong" (p. 7), and welcomed critique of TES. I found this an incredibly refreshing perspective, but I would add that any critique should be accompanied by a suggestion for a better alternative.

I don't believe TES is wrong, rather I found it, like Checkland's work, theoretically dense and incomplete from a practice perspective. That is, it lacked specific guidance for how to actually apply systems thinking skills to evaluate specific evaluands. Further, it was challenging to link TES to Alkin's criteria for an evaluation theory. I believe Cabrera and Trochim (2006) themselves may have recognized the limitations of TES as an evaluation theory when they wrote that they hoped TES would be "a framework upon which protocols and practice can be based, spawning new developments in the field" (p. 2). So, this is exactly what I set out to do; to use my systems thinking skills to design an approach for evaluating systems. I knew this was a gap needing filling and the Helmsley evaluation of the cardiac care system was my opportunity.

It seemed reasonable to posit that a theory to guide evaluating systems should be grounded in the very definition of a system; tailored to evaluate the interdependence and emergence system properties. However, learning from authors like Cabrera and Trochim (2006), Checkland (2000), and Davidson (2005) I reasoned that before I could begin evaluating interdependence and emergence it was necessary to first define the evaluand, that is the complex intervention acting as a system. The defined system would serve as the standard of acceptability against which the evaluation of interdependence and emergence could proceed (Green et al., 1980). In other words, you need to know what to evaluate and how it is supposed to operate before you can evaluate whether it is operating as it should. Given this, I reasoned, based on the system definition, that a systems evaluation theory would need to guide the evaluator to accomplish three purposes: Define the complex intervention acting as a system, evaluate system interdependencies, and evaluate the emergent system property.

The next challenge was to begin to methodically link the various system principles I had been applying independently into my emerging conceptual scheme. To do this I linked different system principles with the evaluation purpose I thought they best served. The resulting conceptual scheme is shown in Figure 5.4.

There is a deliberate logic to the three SET steps. As noted earlier, it is important to first make explicit the standard against which the evaluation is conducted. Thus, the first step must be to define the system, that is the complex intervention acting as a system. Having established the standard of acceptability, it then becomes possible to evaluate system interdependence and emergence, but which should come first, and why? Since the interdependence of system parts is a necessary prerequisite for the

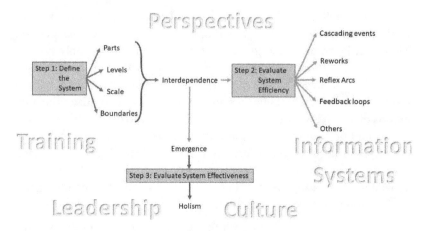

Figure 5.4 The original conceptual scheme underpinning SET.

system property to emerge, I reasoned that evaluating interdependence must precede evaluating emergence. If the evaluation could not establish that the correct mix and balance of interdependent parts are present and operating as intended, then the wisdom of making investments in evaluating the system's emergent property would be questionable.

There are two additional subtleties in Figure 5.4 to which I would like to draw your attention. First, notice that Step 2 leaves room for "other" system principles. This is purposeful, because there are undoubtedly many system principles whose potential in guiding the evaluation of system interdependencies have yet to be discovered and can be subsumed in Step 2 without disrupting the SET's validity and utility. Second, you will notice that I attempt to depict the omnipresence of the four system attributes and the notion of perspectives using a background shadowing effect.

> Over the years I received pushback about the use of my terms system efficiency and effectiveness, most notably from my critical friend Brian Keogh. I have come to realize these terms bring with them the baggage of program evaluation. In hindsight I would have relabeled these steps evaluating interdependence and emergence to avoid these semantic arguments. Nevertheless, it is my contention that asking the questions "Are we doing things right?" (a question related to efficiency) and "Are we doing the right things?" (a question related to effectiveness) apply equally to whether the evaluand is a program or a complex intervention acting as a system.

Validating the Conceptual Scheme
  i. Alignment with other systems models.
    a. The Iceberg Model.

In the previous chapter I introduced you to the Haines iceberg model. The iceberg model is a conceptual model for organizing the relationship between several essential system elements such as the system structures, processes, culture, training, and so forth. Although I came across the Haines model after formulating SET, I felt the model served to validate SET: a pseudo-type of convergent validity. Figure 5.5 shows the relationship between several SET elements and the iceberg profile. The advantage of SET relative to the iceberg profile is that it provides a methodical way of operationalizing the key system elements in the iceberg profile to conduct an evaluation.

    b. Alignment With Checkland's work.

SET's conceptual scheme also closely aligns with the system thinking, systems practice (STSP) and soft systems methodology in action (SSMA) work by Checkland and his colleagues (Checkland, 1981, 2000; Checkland & Scholes, 1990). For example, Checkland (2000) differentiates between hard and soft systems; the former being the structure of the evaluand, the latter being a process of inquiry, that is, system thinking itself. SET uses soft system processes to define the hard system. SET is also philosophically aligned with STSP in that it intentionally "avoids the reductionism of natural science" (p. S12). Finally, SET mirrors some of the key steps in soft systems methodology, for example capturing the complexity of relationships and analyses. The parallels to

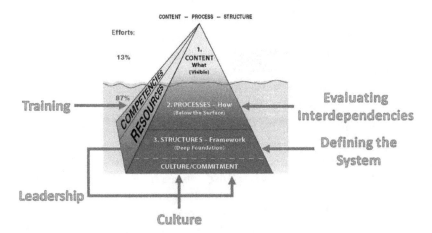

Figure 5.5   SET elements (gray) in relation to the iceberg profile.

Checkland's work provided me additional confidence that SET's conceptual schema was on solid footing!

_____

2. Meeting Alkin's Second Criterion: Applying Set in Other Contexts

All theories, including evaluation theories, must be vetted (Cabrera & Trochim, 2006). I began by testing whether SET could be reliably used to guide evaluations of the same system in different contexts. That is, I began by establishing the usefulness of SET in guiding the evaluations of other cardiac care systems in other states. Even though the cardiac care system emergent property is the same across states, the types of agencies and the way they coordinate differs, providing a good first level test of SET's robustness.

To test SET's robustness, I drew on my experience as a Federal Emergency Management Agency (FEMA) trained master exercise practitioner and began planning, conducting, and evaluating a series of full-scale SCA exercises (Figure 5.6). Each full-scale exercise begins by meeting with stakeholders to define the cardiac care system boundaries, its parts, their interdependencies, and the emergent system property. Then after several months of planning, a cardiac arrest is simulated, and the system actors respond as they would in real time. However, one advantage of an exercise, as opposed to a real-world event, is that the exercise can be slowed down or paused providing the opportunity for evaluators to make inquiries at the time and place where the evaluation observation was made.

I used SET to plan and evaluate a total of seven full-scale exercises in four states. Each time, SET helped ensure that I hadn't missed any key system parts and their interdependencies. Each time, SET led to meaningful system improvements. Over 300 lives were saved as a result of the system improvements. This gave me some initial confidence that SET's conceptual scheme was well grounded.

Since publishing SET, I have successfully used it to evaluate cancer screening systems for underinsured and uninsured women, a multi-state center for translational research, food safety systems, and in a real time COVID-19 emergency response. Others have applied SET to evaluating water scarcity programs (Odgers et al., 2021) and institutional accreditation (Paquibut, 2017). It has been used to guide work in developing whole of school approaches for effective change (Daly-Smith et al., 2020), within the inspector general's office (Inspector-General

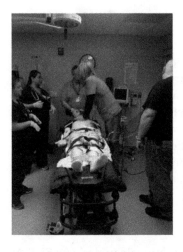
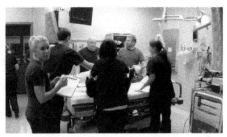

Figure 5.6 Testing SET's conceptual scheme using direct observation during simulated full-scale SCA exercises.

for Emergency Management, 2019), and in the evaluation of boarding school policies (Guenther et al., 2020). At the time of writing this book, I am exploring SET's utility in evaluating homelessness initiatives.

---

3. Meeting Alkin's Third Criterion: Defining Data Collection Strategies and Methods for Each System Evaluation Theory Step

With the considerable investment being made in each full-scale exercise (i.e., exercises ranged in cost from $50,000 to $125,000), I was especially mindful of the need to maximize evaluation learning. Therefore, after each full-scale exercise our evaluation team met and made refinements to the methods used to implement each SET step. For example, we adapted a method called process flow mapping for defining the system operating procedures of the system parts (Renger et al., 2016) and adapted additional Homeland Security exercises (U.S. Department of Homeland Security, 2007a, 2007b, 2013) like the tabletop exercise, to identify and ideally even resolve some potential interdependency problems before the full-scale exercise (Renger et al., 2021).

In their meta-review of evaluation articles employing systems thinking approaches, McGill et al. (2020) concluded that

> although the evaluations identified in this body of literature drew on a range of qualitative methods, with many evaluators using a mix of

qualitative methods within one evaluation design, it was often unclear why certain methods were chosen and the value added by each method. (p. 15)

Each of SET's three steps has a clear purpose and the system thinking principles best able to help complete that step are defined. Chapter 6 details the methods for Step 1 of SET, defining the system. In Chapters 7 and 8, I share the system principles needed to evaluate system interdependencies and how they are applied, respectively (SET Step 2). Chapter 9 is devoted to describing the strategies needed for evaluating system emergence (SET Step 3).

Conclusion

In this chapter, I detailed the history and rationale underlying SET. As evaluators we must be held accountable for being able to explain the "Why?" behind the evaluation theories and methods we use. Knowing why leads to a deeper level of cognitive processing, improved retention, and a better ability to transfer and adapt knowledge to a new setting (e.g., Jeong & Frye, 2018; Weinstein & Macdonald, 1986). These abilities in turn are central to delivering high quality evaluations and by extension will improve our credibility.

In a meta-review of system evaluation McGill et al. (2020) concluded that evaluations "from a complex systems perspective are frequently underdeveloped and poorly specified" (pp. 15–16). SET is my attempt to remedy this reality. The rationale underlying SET is steeped in systems thinking and is consistent with work on systems and system thinking that predated SET. The value added of SET is that it bridges theory and practice, and that should be the ultimate standard by which the utility of any theory is judged (Weiss, 1995).

A useful theory must also be robust. One of the early criticisms of SET came from a good friend of mine, Andrew Hawkins, who argued that SET worked great in the evaluation of the cardiac care system because the interdependencies and system's emergent property were clearly defined (A. Hawkins, personal communication, June 15, 2020). Andrew questioned whether SET had utility in evaluating other more complex systems. My rebuttal to Andrew was that the testing of every theory has a starting point and that the emergency response setting had birthed SET. None of the steps or the sequential application of systems principles that made the cardiac care system seem so obvious and clear to Andrew were so when I began. Only through painstaking work, time, repeated testing, and financial support was I able to make the complex comprehensible. Of course, the next step is continuing to test SET in other contexts, and, as discussed above, that process is well underway.

Like Cabrera and Trochim (2006), I recognize that the current version of SET has a shelf-life. However, it is my hope that SET lays the groundwork necessary to make further advancements in evaluating systems, whether that be refining SET, for example by adding additional systems principles, or perhaps creating an entirely new approach for evaluating systems.

References

Agency for Healthcare Research and Quality. (2021). *TeamSTEPPS fundamentals course: Module 6. Mutual Support.* https://www.ahrq.gov/team stepps/instructor/fundamentals/module6/igmutualsupp.html

Alkin, M. C. (1969). Evaluation theory development. *Evaluation Comment, 2*(1), 2–7.

Booze, W., & Weinkauf, S. (2013). *Necessity is the mother of invention: Utilizing technology to provide high quality healthcare to rural areas of the upper Midwest.* The Leona M. and Harry B. Charitable Trust: Rural Healthcare Program.

Cabrera, D., & Trochim, W. M. K. (2006). A theory of systems evaluation. In D. Cabrera (Ed.), *Systems evaluation and evaluation systems whitepaper series.* Cornell University.

Checkland, P. (1981). *Systems thinking, systems practice.* John Wiley & Sons.

Checkland, P. (2000). Soft systems methodology: A thirty-year retrospective. *Systems Research and Behavioral Science, 17,* 11–58.

Checkland, P., & Scholes, J. (1990). *Soft systems methodology in action.* Wiley.

Christie, C. A., & Alkin, M. C. (2013). An evaluation theory tree. In C. A. Christie & M. C. Alkin (Eds.), *Evaluation roots: A wider perspective of theorists' views and influences* (2nd ed., pp. 11–57). SAGE Publications.

Cummins, R. O., Eisenberg, M. S., Hallstrom, A. P., & Liwin, P. E. (1985). Survival of out-of-hospital cardiac arrest with early initiation of cardiopulmonary resuscitation. *American Journal of Emergency Medicine, 3*(2), 114–119. https://doi.org/10.1016/0735-6757(85)90032-4

Daly-Smith, A., Quarmby, T., Archbold, V. S. J., Corrigan, N., Wilson, D., Resaland, G. K., Bartholomew, J. B., Singh, A., Tjomsland, H. E., Sherar, L. B., Chalkley, A., Routen, A. C., Shickle, D., Bingham, D. D., Barber, S. E., van Sluijs, E., Fairclough, S. J., & McKenna, J. (2020). Using a multi-stakeholder experience-based design process to co-develop the creating active schools framework. *International Journal of Behavioral Nutrition and Physical Activity, 17*(13). https://doi.org/10.1186/s12966-020-0917-z

Davidson, J. (2005). *Evaluation methodology basics: The nuts and bolts of sound evaluation.* SAGE Publications.

Green, L. W., Kreuter, M. W., Deeds, S. G., Partridge, K. B., & Bartlett, E. (1980). *Health education planning: A diagnostic approach.* Mayfield Publishing.

Guenther, J., Benvensite, T., Redman-MacLaren, M., Mander, D., McCalman, J., O'Bryan, M., Osborne, S., & Stewrat, R. (2020). Thinking with theory as a policy evaluation tool: The case of boarding schools for remote First Nations students. *Evaluation Journal of Australasia, 20*(1), 34–52. https://doi.org/10.1177/1035719X20905056

Inspector-General for Emergency Management. (2019). *Critical infrastructure resilience: 2018 report.* https://files.igem.vic.gov.au/2021-03/Critical%20Infrastructure%20Resilience%202018%20Report.PDF

Jeong, J., & Frye, D. (2018). Explicit versus implicit understanding of teaching: Does knowing what teaching is help children to learn from it? *Teaching and Teacher Education, 71,* 355–365. https://doi.org/10.1016/j.tate.2018.02.002

McGill, E., Marks, D., Er, V., Penney, T., Petticrew, M., & Egan, M. (2020). Qualitative process evaluation from a complex system perspective: A systematic review and framework for public health evaluators. *PLoS Med, 17*(11), e1003368. https://doi.org/10.1371/journal.pmed.1003368

Mcshane, S., & Von Glinow, M. (2009). *Organizational behavior: Emerging knowledge and practice for the real world* (5th ed.). McGraw Hill.

Mertens, D. M., & Wilson, A. T. (2019). *Program evaluation theory and practice: A comprehensive guide* (2nd ed.). The Guilford Press.

Odgers, J., Johnson, B., Keogh, B., Rutherford, J., Alexandra, J., & Hawkins, A. (2021, February 24). *Environmental water management program 2014–2019 evaluation.* NSW Dept of Planning, Industry, & Environment. https://www.environment.nsw.gov.au/-/media/OEH/Corporate-Site/Documents/Water/Water-for-the-environment/environmental-water-management-program-evaluation-2014-19.pdf

Olasveengen, T. M., Vik, E., Kuzovlev, A., & Sunde, K. (2009). Effect of implementation of new resuscitation guidelines on quality of cardio-pulmonary resuscitation and survival. *Resuscitation, 80*(4), 407–411. https://doi.org/10.1016/j.resuscitation.2008.12.005

Paquibut, R. Y. (2017). A systems evaluation theory analyzing value and re-sults chain for institutional accreditation in Oman. *Quality Assurance in Education, 25*(2), 161–170.

Renger, R. (2015). System evaluation theory (SET): A practical frame-work for evaluators to meet the challenges of system evaluation. *Evaluation Journal of Australasia, 15*(4), 16–28. https://doi.org/10 .1177/1035719X1501500403

Renger, R., McPherson, M., Kontz-Bartels, T., & Becker, K. (2016). Process flow mapping for systems improvement: Lessons learned. *The Cana-dian Journal of Program Evaluation, 31*, 109–121.

Renger, R., Renger, J., Basson, M. D., Van Eck, R., Renger, J., Souvannasacd, E., & Hart, G. (2021). Using the Homeland Security and Exercise Evaluation Program (HSEEP) building block approach to imple-ment system evaluation theory (SET). *American Journal of Evaluation, 42*(4), 586–601 https://doi.org/10.1177/1098214020986619

Sinek, S. (2009). *Start with the why: How great leaders inspire everyone to take action.* Penguin.

Sweet, P. (2017, July 4). *The importance of knowing your "why."* https://engi-neeringmanagementinstitute.org/knowing-your-why/

U.S. Department of Homeland Security. (2007a). *Homeland security exercise and evaluation program: Volume I: HSEEP overview and exercise program management.* https://www.ojp.gov/pdffiles1/Archive/205244NCJRS .pdf

U.S. Department of Homeland Security. (2007b). *Homeland security exercise and evaluation program: Volume III: Exercise evaluation and improvement planning.* https://www.hsdl.org/?view&did=470613

U.S. Department of Homeland Security. (2013). *Homeland security and exer-cise evaluation program.* https://www.hsdl.org/?view&did=735311

Von Bertalanffy, L. (1972). The history and status of general systems theo-ry. *The Academy of Management Journal, 15*(4), 407–426. www.jstor.org/ stable/255139

Weinstein. C. E., & Macdonald, J. D. (1986). Why does a school psycholo-gist need to know about learning strategies. *Journal of School Psycholo-gy, 24*(3), 257–265. https://doi.org/10.1016/0022-4405(86)90058-0

Weiss, C. H. (1995). Nothing as practical as a good theory: Exploring the-ory-based evaluation for comprehensive community initiatives for children and families. In J. P. Connell, A. C. Kubisch, L. B. Schorr, & C. H. Weiss (Eds.), *New approaches to evaluating community initiatives* (pp. 65–69). Aspen Institute.

Williams, B. (2010). *Fitting the key to the lock: Matching systems methods to evaluation questions.* The 24th annual conference of the American Evaluation Association, San Antonio, Texas, United States.

Yang, Z., Heng, L., Tao, Y., Changwei, C., & Zitong, H. (2013). The quality of hands-only CPR deteriorates in one minute but without subjective fatigue of the rescuer. *Critical Care Medicine, 41*(12), A117. https://doi.org/10.1097/01.ccm.0000439624.18671.92

Yannopoulos, D., Aufderheide, T. P., Abella, B. S., Duval, S., Frascone, R. J., Goodloe, J. M., Mahoney, B. D., Nadkarni, V. M., Halperin, H. R., O'Connor, R., Idris, A. H., Becker, L. B., & Pepe, P. E. (2015). Quality of CPR: An important effect modifier in cardiac arrest clinical outcomes and intervention effectiveness trials. *Resuscitation, 94*, 106–113. https://doi.org/10.1016/j.resuscitation.2015.06.004

Yunkaporta, T. (2020). *Sand talk: How indigenous thinking can save the world.* Harper One.

6

System Evaluation Theory Step 1, Defining the Complex Intervention Acting as a System

Renger evaluation mantra: Why, what, how ... in that order.

Now that you understand the *why* behind system evaluation theory ([SET]; Renger, 2015), it's time to begin to learn *how* to apply SET. This chapter focuses on the first step, defining the complex intervention acting as a system. The term system is used throughout this chapter and is shorthand for the complex intervention acting as a system.

There are several things we are trying to define in this first step including the system boundaries, system parts, their interdependencies, and the emergent system property, but not necessarily in that order. It is important to remember that when we define the system, we are taking a snapshot of a system that is dynamic; that is, it is functioning and changing every minute. Once defined, we then apply our system thinking principles to evaluate the system as it is actually operating. McGill et

System Evaluation Theory, pages 97–116
Copyright © 2022 by Information Age Publishing
www.infoagepub.com
97

al. (2020) refers to the snapshot phase where the system is defined as the "static system description" (p. 16) and the evaluation phase as the "analysis of the system undergoing change" (p. 17). This is an important concept because contrary to the belief that for an evaluation judgment to be rendered the intervention implementation must remain true to its original design, the reality is that a highly functioning complex intervention will evolve, constantly trying to improve in how it meets clients' needs.

You will be introduced to a seven-step process for defining a complex intervention acting as a system (see Figure 6.1). The product of the seven steps is a visual representation of "the system structure and boundaries to help depict and understand the system structure and relationships between the system elements" (McGill, 2020, p. 18). The seven steps are steeped in systems thinking. That is, as you complete a step you may learn new information requiring you to loop back to be sure you understand how that impacts your previous understanding of the system. So even though I present the steps sequentially, know that in reality you may have to revisit steps several times in an iterative manner, so be sure to maintain an ongoing learning orientation.

As I explain how to complete each step, I illustrate their application to two systems: a restaurant system and the cardiac care system with which by now you know was the proving ground for SET. The restaurant operates at a lower, staff level, while the cardiac care example operates at a higher agency level. I use these two examples to help you understand that the steps for defining the system are the same regardless of the system level (Chapter 3) or its complexity.

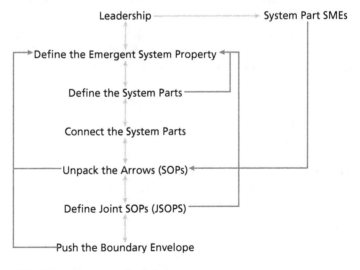

Figure 6.1   The seven-steps in defining a system.

At the end of each step, I provide key evaluation decision points. The evaluation decision points are based on my personal experience in defining complex interventions acting as systems and are intended to assist evaluation practitioners in knowing what to do given a particular outcome of a step.

Completing the seven-steps is heavily dependent on the evaluator's facilitation skills (Morabito, 2002). Being an effective and respectful communicator is one of the evaluator competencies (Canadian Evaluation Society, 2018). Even though there are manuals developed to help you become a competent facilitator, much of it comes down to your personality (Birch-Jones & Kent, 2011). And to be honest, not all evaluators are cut out to be good facilitators; while it can be learned, much of it is innate. Therefore, I would recommend ensuring that whoever takes on the facilitator role in your evaluation is adept at this skill.

The Seven Steps to Defining a Complex Intervention Operating and Functioning as a System.

Step 1: Get Leaders to the Table and Ensure You Have Buy-In

As you learned in Chapter 4, leadership is the key to making a system work. Leadership buy-in in particular is critical to securing the cooperation and resources necessary to implement the evaluation plan as well as leveraging the resources needed to implement evaluation recommendations for improving system efficiency and effectiveness. Given the importance of leadership buy-in, naturally, the first step in defining a complex intervention acting as a system is to bring leadership to the table (Figure 6.2). So, who is/are the leader(s)? While there is considerable literature on what constitutes a leader such as the differences between leading and managing (Turk, 2007) and group versus individual leadership (Hoyt et al., 2003), in practice, the *leader is the person who is the ultimate decision-maker*. That person usually controls the money and decides whether to implement the evaluation recommendations!

Figure 6.2 Meeting with EMS leadership in Aberdeen SD, to define the cardiac system of care.

In my experience, there's a 50–50 chance that your first contact with the system will be with the leader. There is also a good chance that the person reaching out to you for evaluation support was asked to do so by someone else. So, if I don't have a key decision-maker(s) at the table, my first request is that the leader(s) become part of the evaluation process.

Leadership willing to participate?
No: Perhaps consider not pursuing the evaluation.

If leadership is not present or willing to come to the table, then it might be a good indicator (see system evaluation readiness scan [SERS], Chapter 4) that pursuing the evaluation is not in anyone's best interest. As I noted earlier in the book, I realize your ability to turn down work depends on your circumstance. I couldn't imagine early in my career, hungry for work, placing any contingencies on getting a contract. With career stability, I have the luxury of declining work so it's easier for me to insist leaders be at the table, or I walk. Agreeing to do the evaluation is about more than money, it's about my own integrity, honesty, and respect for my client (Morris, 2011). I know without leadership buy-in the evaluation will have little to no utility, period. You need to work in alignment to your own core values, but I would encourage you to ask yourself the question, "Would it be ethical to proceed knowing that without leaders at the table the evaluation is likely to fail?"

> In the restaurant system, leadership could include the manager, person-in-charge, and/or the owner.

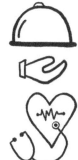

> In the cardiac care system, leadership included the state emergency medical services director and/or chief medical officer.

Step 2: Define the Emergent System Property

The successful operation and function of a complex intervention acting as a system hinges on leaders and actors having a shared understanding of what they are trying to accomplish. Recall from Chapter 2 that if system parts are truly interdependent, then the failure of just one system part to share in this understanding can have disastrous effects.

> I'm sure many of you reading this have been required to complete some form of group work. Groups whose members have a shared understanding of collective success, such as social well-being, perform much better than those who have members narrowly focused on academic success (Volet & Mansfield, 2006). In fact, as a professor for 23 years, I have seen the lack of a shared understanding of a clear purpose result in group members engaging in sabotage, even to their own detriment!

In my experience, there are two major challenges in defining the emergent system property. The first is that leaders and actors are unlikely, initially, to understand the concept of an emergent system property. Using "academic" sounding terms risks the process being viewed "as unrelated to the rough and tumble of practical affairs"

(Checkland, 2000, p. S13). Robert Grimshaw, a workshop participant from the Australian Tax Office, once asked me what types of questions I ask clients to be able to guide them in defining the system emergent property, without using the term itself. Together we derived the following list:

- "If everything in the system is working as it should, what would it produce?"
- "What is our collective purpose?"
- "What does the coalition/partnership/cooperative hope to achieve together that individual agencies can't do alone?"
- "What do your staff hope to accomplish that they can't achieve alone?"
- "What is the common, overarching goal?"

When needed, I will help facilitate the discussion of an emergent property by drawing on Ackoff's car example (Chapter 2). I've also had success in using a sports example to explain emergence. That is, in team sports, cohesion is an emergent property necessary for success (Senécal et al., 2008). If a player has individual aspirations, rather than being committed to a shared team goal, then cohesion and collective efficacy suffer (Widmeyer & Ducharme, 1997).

Opening the discussion with an overarching question about what the complex intervention acting as a system is accomplishing and whether this differs from what it is intended to collectively accomplish is a good way to gauge the extent to which there is agreement on the emergent system property (Bang et al., 2010).

The second challenge is getting *consensus* on the emergent system property. Research consistently shows that in organizational systems there is often "no stable consensus" among system actors (Yuchtman & Seashore, 1967). I am a seasoned cynic so I am no longer surprised when I learn of the degree of disparity in understanding about what is trying to be accomplished between people working on the same initiative, sometimes together for decades. To no one's surprise the disparity is often the greatest between leadership and the actors responsible for day-to-day systems operations. In fact, this disparity formed the basis for the popular television show *Undercover Boss*.

A colleague of mine, Mark Beevers working for the Inspector-General for Emergency Management was tasked to define the emergent system property for the emergency management system. Mark didn't have the luxury of time and was working with limited resources. His clever solution was to turn to the law which gave EM its authorization. That law clearly articulated EM's overarching purpose/goal to save property and lives. This served as a better starting point for Mark to gain consensus about the system's emergent property.

Recall from your SERS that the lack of agreement may be an indicator of broader organizational cultural problems. Therefore, if you proceed with the evaluation, then you will have to determine a method for dealing with the cultural barriers. I describe one approach to mitigate such a challenge in Step 5.

Consensus on emergent system property?
No: Consider not moving forward until you do.

In the restaurant system, the emergent system property might be something like customer satisfaction as evaluated by return customers.

> In the cardiac care system, the emergent system property is improved quality of life as measured by survival rate and improved neurological outcomes.

Step 3: Define the System Parts

Recall from Chapter 2, that system parts include a set of plans, resources, authorities, agencies, and their associated human resources (Jackson et al., 2012). Instead of an open discussion about who and all that is involved in the system, I ask leaders to define the parts that are needed for the essential system property to emerge. I then write all the system parts down on a whiteboard, or virtually using tools such as Zoom and PowerPoint.

In Step 5, you will need the perspectives of those intimately familiar with how each system part works. So, while I have access to the leaders, I ask them to identify system part subject matter experts (SMEs), that is, system actors with lived experiences in the day-to-day system operations. In the restaurant system, it is the manager (not necessarily the owner) who is most familiar with the day-to-day operations and the interplay between staff, equipment, and technology. In the cardiac care system, SMEs were needed from each agency involved in the coordinated response.

Are the perspectives of all the system parts included?
No: Ask leadership to identify perspectives and return to Step 2.

The parts include the staff, equipment, and product (e.g., bread, top-pings) needed to deliver a quality product so the customer will be satisfied.

The parts are the response agencies needing to coordinate for the quality of life to emerge.

Step 4: Connect the Parts

If leadership is confident that all system parts are represented, then the next step is to connect the parts to reflect their interdependencies. This step mirrors that of Checkland (2000) and is a simple exercise of connecting arrows. Again, I typically will facilitate this in a face-to-face meeting using a whiteboard, or virtually using tools such as Zoom and PowerPoint.

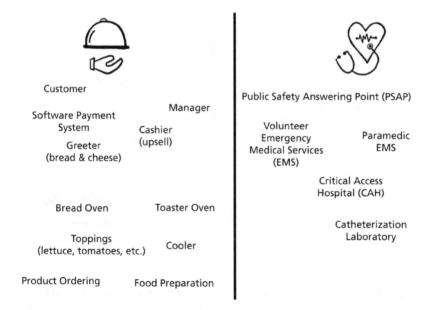

Figure 6.3 The parts of two different systems reflect the level at which the system is being evaluated.

Once the parts are connected, I draw a line around them to depict the system boundary created for evaluation purposes (see Figure 6.4). I draw the boundary using a dotted line. This is a purposeful reminder that I have created a system for evaluation purposes (Wolski, 2020), that is open (Chapter 2), and not operating in isolation from the rest of the world (McFadden, 2018).

System boundaries naturally emanate from an understanding of the systems parts needed for the essential system property to emerge. In fact, I find it quite unhelpful to begin any conversation with clients by trying to establish the system boundaries, I instead allow the boundaries to naturally evolve by defining the system parts.

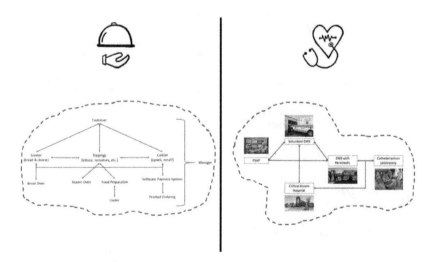

Figure 6.4 Connecting system parts reflect their interdependencies and simultaneously define the system boundary.

Step 5: Unpack the Arrows: Define the System Operating Procedures

It is important to realize that while the connecting arrows represent system part interdependencies, there is much more going on inside an arrow that needs to be unpacked; we need to know what the arrows mean (Williams, 2014). In my earlier work I referred to this detail as the *standard* operating procedure, but I have altered my language slightly and now refer to them as *system* operating procedures (SOPs). I think the latter term serves as a reminder that the focus needs to be broadened from how an individual part operates, to how it operates in concert with other parts.

From an evaluation perspective SOPs are important because the detailed operating steps they contain form the standard against which to evaluate success (Green & Kreuter, 2005). As I wrote earlier, you need to know how system parts are intended to operate together, before you can evaluate whether they are in fact working as intended.

As part of my SERS (Chapter 4), I enquire whether the system has their processes documented. This helps me in several regards. First, it gives me a sense of where my client is on the continuum of systems thinking. It is easier to move clients along who appreciate the importance of, and have already invested in, developing SOPs. Second, it will save the client time and money to build on existing investments rather than to start from scratch. This is, afterall, what the evaluation feasibility standard is all about (Yarbrough et al., 2010). Third, by building on existing SOPs, it demonstrates to the client that they already have made important systems thinking investments, making them more open to continuing with a systems approach to evaluation.

In my experience, complex interventions acting as systems vary greatly in the extent to which their SOPs have the detail needed for evaluation purposes. On the one end of the continuum, medical systems like hospitals, often have very detailed SOPs; they call them workflows. The importance of standardizing care and the all too frequent medical malpractice lawsuits makes SOPs in the medical field an imperative. Similarly, chain restaurants, like Subway and McDonalds, also have detailed SOPs, and refer to them as such ("Subway Job Descriptions," n.d.). They invest in SOPs to ensure the customer experience is consistent across franchises, because a negative experience at one location impacts all locations.

In my experience, most complex interventions acting as a system lie on the opposite end of the continuum, they have nothing documented as to how they operate. When I encounter this situation, I need to define the SOPs. I use a method called process flow mapping (PFM) to achieve this purpose (Renger et al., 2016). I complete the PFM with the SMEs identified by leaders in Step 3.

> Sometimes getting leadership to invest in documenting SOPs, when they do not have them, is challenging. One strategy I use to help move the needle is to point out that SOPs are also helpful in standardizing training. Pointing out that SOPs have a benefit to the system beyond conducting the evaluation often removes this barrier to cooperation.

I prefer to do the PFM in person, using a whiteboard (see Figure 6.5). However, as the pandemic forced me to learn, you can complete a PFM virtually by sharing a PowerPoint screen. The SOP can normally be documented in about 60–90 minutes, provided the facilitator is skilled in this process (see Figure 6.6).

After the PFM session is complete, I conduct a member check by creating a summary consisting of the process flow diagram and a short narrative highlighting some key aspects of the process as shared by the

Figure 6.5 Conducting a PFM as part of the cardiac care system evaluation.

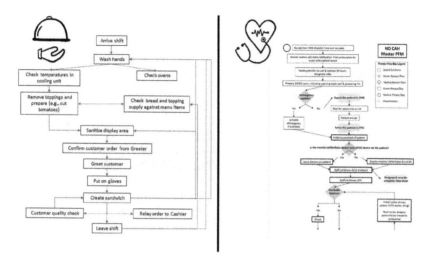

Figure 6.6 A restaurant SOP for the topping station and part of an SOP for a Critical Access Hospital in the Cardiac Care System.

interviewees (Renger & Bourdeau, 2004). I then send the summary to the SME for validation.

Do the SOPs reveal missing system parts?
If so, return to Step 2 and repeat the process.

Step 6: Bring Groups Together to Define Joint System Operating Procedures.

The sequence in which you define SOPs is important. I recommend following the Homeland Security and Exercise Evaluation Program building block design (see Figure 6.7) to define SOPs (Renger et al., 2021; U.S. Department of Homeland Security, 2007a, 2007b, 2013). The philosophy underpinning the building block design is to work out as

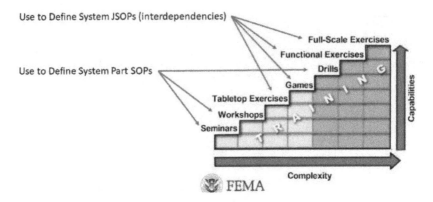

Figure 6.7 The relationship between the HSEEP building block design and defining SOPs & JSOPs.

much of the system detail through discussion (i.e., under minimal or no stress and with less costs) before using operations-based exercises to test the system under time constraints (i.e., more stress and greater costs).

The first building block exercise is the *seminar* and its purpose is to raise awareness around an issue, like the need for an emergency plan. This is followed by a *workshop*, the goal of which is to produce a written product, like the emergency plan. The seminar and workshop are completed with individual agencies. The next exercise is the table *top exercise* (TTx), in which different agencies are brought together to understand how their workshop products must be adjusted to accommodate other agencies. A frequent product of a TTx are memorandums of understanding and agreement. When as many kinks as possible have been ironed out through discussion, then it is recommended to move to *operations-based exercises* to see how the agreements play out under real world conditions. A *drill* is recommended for individual agencies to test their emergency plans. This is then followed by a *functional exercise* in which all the agencies simulate a real-world event. Finally, a *full-scale exercise* is used when the plans and agreements are tested in real time.

In evaluation practice, I use the seminar to introduce what the system evaluation is trying to accomplish and to begin an orientation to systems thinking. My goal is to include as many system actors as possible in the seminar. This helps me understand their role and improves evaluation buy-in at all system levels. Again, the more people that understand the why, the more motivated they will be to cooperate (Sweet, 2017). I then conduct a workshop using the PFM exercise to document each system part's SOP. Working with actors from each system part individually helps me to better understand their perspectives and how they relate to the whole. This helps me better appreciate the system's level of complexity, which will ultimately lead to a better understanding of which system interdependencies are most vulnerable to failure. This allows me to better allocate my finite evaluation resources and results towards more meaningful recommendations.

Once the SOPs for each system part are defined, it's time to begin to define how the parts coordinate. I start by using a TTx. To do this I develop a PowerPoint presentation of a typical system scenario (e.g., in the restaurant system this could be serving a customer). I then walk slowly through each process step, providing an opportunity for each system part representative to reflect on whether changes to their SOP need to be made to accommodate another system part. This format is very useful in having individual system parts/people gain an appreciation for each other and the impact their decisions have on the other parts/people and the emergent system property.

When facilitating a system discussion, consider adopting Dr. Lewe Atkinson's Rubik's cube analogy to get things going. Assign each system part one side of the cube and ask them to make their side all one color. This is quite simple to do, but what becomes immediately evident is the consequences of each movement on the other five sides of the cube. Thus demonstrating that individual parts cannot work in isolation without negatively impacting the systems as a whole.

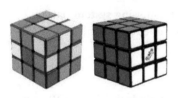

When as much of the interaction detail is worked out through discussion as possible, I consider adapting additional operations-based exercises to further refine the Joint-SOPs (JSOPs). I prefer full-scale exercises because they are more realistic and more engaging for the system actors than the functional exercise. However, full-scale exercises are time consuming and expensive. Under conditions of limited time and money you might consider a functional exercise, which is a simulation of the real-world event.

The TTx brings all the staff together and presents them with scenarios that impact the emergent system property: customer satisfaction. For example, what happens if one staff member is called away for a family emergency, or what if the customer changes his/her mind, and so on? A full-scale exercise might take the form of someone role playing a customer and the staff working through the scenario in real time.

Workshops were used to develop SOPs for each system part. A TTx exercise with representation for each response agency was used to revise JSOPs. Full-scale exercises were then run to understand further how JSOPs might need to be adjusted to accommodate each other.

Do the refined JSOPs suggest a missing system part?
If so, return to Step 2 and repeat the process.

Step 7: Push the Boundary Envelope

Having defined the system parts, their individual SOPs, and the JSOPs, I then present the findings to leadership to close the loop. I engage leaders in an exercise I coined "push the boundary envelope" (see Figure 6.8). Remember, the boundaries are *created* boundaries for evaluation purposes (Wolski, 2020). As a result of defining JSOPs, it may be the case that system boundary adjustments are warranted, either to include a missing system part and/or remove an unnecessary redundancy. This is where I implement the Renger Check-mix rule; I simply ask leaders whether there is any system part that needs to be included that is not within the system boundary and whether redundant system parts within the boundary are necessary.

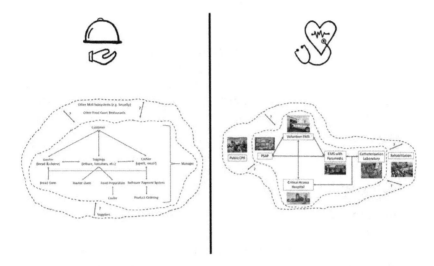

Figure 6.8 Pushing the boundary envelopes of the restaurant and cardiac care systems.

Did the boundaries change?
If yes, repeat Steps 2–7.

Expanding the system boundary might mean including higher level systems, such as the food court, the mall, or the city tourism. Each level possesses the same emergent property (i.e., customer satisfaction), but the interdependencies reflect qualitatively different relationships at each level (Chapter 3).

> When I pushed the boundary envelope, leaders considered whether to include the next upstream subsystems (i.e., school cardiopulmonary resuscitation) and/or downstream (i.e., cardiac rehabilitation). In the end, leadership decided that even though these parts contribute to the emergent system property (i.e., quality of life) they fell outside of the response itself.

Conclusion

Defining the complex intervention acting as a system is an iterative process underpinned by systems thinking. It is a resource intensive process; as is any evaluation process that meaningfully integrates stakeholder input. As you complete a step you may learn something that requires you to loop back and revisit previous steps. This can be a tedious and time-consuming process, but the success of the evaluation rests on having this foundation in place. Don't give up and shortcut this process! You will reap the rewards later with recommendations that are much more likely to be adopted.

The two illustrative examples in the chapter differ in the system level being defined. The restaurant was at a staff level, while the cardiac care example was at an agency level. Regardless of the system level, the steps of defining the system are the same and deliver the same end product, JSOPs. In the next chapter you will learn how to apply systems principles to evaluate the efficiency of these JSOPs.

References

Bang, H., Fuglesang, S. L., Ovesen, M. R., & Eilertsen, D. E. (2010). Effectiveness in top management group meetings: The role of goal clarity, focused communication, and learning behavior. *Scandinavian Journal of Psychology, 51*, 253–261. https://doi.org/10.1111/j.1467-9450.2009.00769.x

Birch-Jones, J., & Kent, J. (2011). *Facilitation skills for evaluators.* IPDET. https://citeseerx.ist.psu.edu/viewdoc/download?doi=10.1.1.364.7674&rep=rep1&type=pdf

Canadian Evaluation Society. (2018). *Competencies for Canadian evaluation practice.* https://evaluationcanada.ca/txt/2_competencies_cdn_evaluation_practice_2018.pdf

Checkland, P. (2000). Soft systems methodology: A thirty-year retrospective. *Systems Research and Behavioral Science, 17,* 11–58.

Green, L., & Kreuter, M. (2005). *Health program planning: An educational and ecological approach* (4th ed.). McGraw Hill.

Hoyt, C. L., Murphy, S. E., Halverson, S. K., & Watson, C. B. (2003). Group leadership: Efficacy and effectiveness. *Group Dynamics: Theory, Research, and Practice, 7*(4), 259–274. https://doi.org/10.1037/1089-2699.7.4.259

Jackson, B. A., Faith, K. S., & Willis, H. H. (2012). Evaluating the reliability of emergency response systems for large-scale incident operations. *Rand Health Quarterly, 2*(3), 8.

McFadden, M. (2018). *Systems thinking for 21st century cities: A beginner's introduction—Part #2. How city systems, boundaries, and lenses relate to wicked problems.* Medium. https://medium.com/@meganmcfadden/systems-thinking-for-21st-century-cities-a-beginners-introduction-part-2-f4c1278a2d7e

McGill, E., Marks, D., Er, V., Penney, T., Petticrew, M., & Egan, M. (2020). Qualitative process evaluation from a complex system perspective: A systematic review and framework for public health evaluators. *PLoS Med, 17*(11), e1003368. https://doi.org/10.1371/journal.pmed.1003368

Morabito, S. M. (2002). Evaluator roles and strategies for expanding evaluation process influence. *American Journal of Evaluation, 23*(3), 321–330. https://doi.org/10.1177/109821400202300307

Morris, M. (2011). The good, the bad, and the evaluator: 25 years of AJE ethics. *American Journal of Evaluation, 32*(1), 134–151. https://doi.org/10.1177/1098214010388267

Renger, R. (2015). System evaluation theory (SET): A practical framework for evaluators to meet the challenges of system evaluation. *Evaluation Journal of Australasia, 15*(4), 16–28. https://doi.org/10.1177/1035719X1501500403

Renger, R., & Bourdeau, B. (2004). Strategies for values inquiry: An exploratory case study. *American Journal of Evaluation, 25*(1), 39–49. https://doi.org/10.1177%2F109821400402500103

Renger, R., McPherson, M., Kontz-Bartels, T., & Becker, K. (2016). Process flow mapping for systems improvement: Lessons learned. *The Canadian Journal of Program Evaluation, 31,* 109–121.

Renger, R., Renger, J., Basson, M. D., Van Eck, R., Renger, J., Souvannasacd, E., & Hart, G. (2021). Using the Homeland Security and Exercise Evaluation Program (HSEEP) building block approach to implement system evaluation theory (SET). *American Journal of Evaluation, 42*(4), 586–601 https://doi.org/10.1177/1098214020986619

Senécal, J., Lougheed, T. M., & Bloom, G. A. (2008). A season-long team-building intervention: Examining the effect of team goal setting on cohesion. *Journal of Sport and Exercise Psychology, 30,* 186–199. https://doi.org/10.1123/jsep.30.2.186

Subway Job Descriptions. (n.d.). Worknearyou.net. https://worknearyou
  .net/subway-job-descriptions/

Sweet, P. (2017, July 4). *The importance of knowing your "why."* https://
  engineeringmanagementinstitute.org/knowing-your-why/

Turk, W. (2007). Manager or leader? *Defense AT&L, 36*(4), 20–22. https://
  www.dau.edu/library/defense-atl/DATLFiles/2007_07_08/j-a07.pdf

U.S. Department of Homeland Security. (2007a). *Homeland security exercise
  and evaluation program: Volume I: HSEEP overview and exercise program
  management.* https://www.ojp.gov/pdffiles1/Archive/205244NCJRS
  .pdf

U.S. Department of Homeland Security. (2007b). *Homeland security exercise
  and evaluation program: Volume III: Exercise evaluation and improvement
  planning.* https://www.hsdl.org/?view&did=470613

U.S. Department of Homeland Security. (2013). *Homeland security and exercise evaluation program.* https://www.hsdl.org/?view&did=735311

Volet, S. E., & Mansfield, C. (2006). Group work at university: Significance
  of personal goals in the regulation strategies of students with positive
  and negative appraisals. *Higher Education and Research Development,
  25*(4), 341–356. https://doi.org/10.1080/07294360600947301

Widmeyer, W. N., & Ducharme, K. (1997). Team building through team
  goal setting. *Journal of Applied Sport Psychology, 9*(1), 97–113. https://
  doi.org/10.1080/10413209708415386

Williams, B. (2014). *Week 36: Systems thinking.* Better Evaluation. https://
  www.betterevaluation.org/en/blog/systems_thinking

Wolski, M. (2020). *System requirements—The context and boundary of a system.* https://michael.wolski.pro/2018/01/system-requirements-the
  -context-and-boundary-of-the-system/

Yarbrough, D. B., Shula, L. M., Hopson, R. K., & Caruthers, F. A. (2010).
  *The program evaluation standards: A guide for evaluators and evaluation
  users* (3rd ed). Corwin Press.

Yuchtman, E., & Seashore, S. E. (1967). A system resource approach to
  organizational effectiveness. *American Sociological Review, 32*(6), 891–
  903. https://www.jstor.org/stable/2092843

7

System Evaluation Theory Step 2, Evaluating System Efficiency (Interdependencies)

Every system is perfectly designed to get the results it gets.
—Deming, n.d.

If the results are less than desired, the system structures, processes, linkages, and information flows need to be adjusted.
—Haines, 2000

At this point in your systems evaluation, you've defined the complex intervention acting as a system, its parts, and interdependencies. Now that you know *what* you are supposed to evaluate you are ready to learn *how* to evaluate it. Recall from Chapter 5 that system evaluation theory (SET) is a blueprint for how to evaluate a system that is intentionally aligned and sequenced to evaluate the system properties of interdependence and emergence, in that order. This is because interdependence is a necessary prerequisite for the system property to emerge.

System Evaluation Theory, pages 117–140

To evaluate system interdependencies is to evaluate system efficiency. To evaluate system efficiency, you must compare how the system interdependencies are supposed to work, as defined by the system operating procedures (SOPs), with how they are actually executed. I use a variety of mixed methods to make these comparisons, such as direct observation, surveying system actors, analyzing system data, and so forth (Gear et al., 2018).

The complex intervention you are evaluating will, by definition, have numerous moving parts and, by extension, numerous interdependencies. On the safe assumption that you have finite evaluation resources, knowing where to invest them to get the biggest return on investment is critical. SET is helpful in this regard because it guides you to methodically apply several system principles to quickly locate and evaluate those system processes most susceptible to failure; where system parts are connected and depend on each other to function. Some authors have referred to these as "trigger or choke points" (Renger et al., 2017), linkages, "seams" (Jackson et al., 2012), "linchpins," and "handoffs" (Renger, 2016). I refer to them collectively as vulnerable interdependencies.

The three system principles you will learn about in this chapter to evaluate system interdependencies are *feedback loops, cascading failures*, and *reflex arcs*. Each one provides a different way to analyze system interdependencies. Afterall, not all interdependencies manifest themselves the same way. These three system principles are ones that I have found to be incredibly powerful in helping me to dissect and evaluate SOPs. By powerful, I mean that the recommendations arising from the evaluation using these system principles were not just considered, but adopted at about an 80% rate! (Renger et al., 2022).

Some of the system principles to evaluate interdependencies, like feedback loops, may be more familiar to you, while system principles like cascading failures and reflex arcs may be less so. My goal in this chapter is to move you beyond what I find to be dry theoretical discussions of these principles and to show you the power of these system principles in real world application. To do this, I illustrate each of the system principles with examples from my evaluation practice including the COVID-19 pandemic response (Renger, 2021).

System Principles for Evaluating System Interdependencies

Feedback Loops

> A *feedback loop* is a "form of interconnection, present in a wide range of systems." "Feedback may be negative (compensatory or balancing) or positive (exaggerating or reinforcing)" (Ison, 2008, p. 141).

I like Ison's (2008) definition because it is easily operationalized for evaluation purposes. *In practical terms, a feedback loop can occur anywhere and anytime information is exchanged between system parts.* Information exchange can occur between human beings such as in a job performance review, or between technology such as in a health information exchange network, or between human beings and technology such as when a doctor interprets a patient's electrocardiogram (EKG). In an information exchange, one or more system parts depend on each other, therefore to evaluate a feedback loop is to evaluate a type of interdependency.

In my experience the feedback loop is one of the most frequently occurring and easiest system principles to apply in evaluation. Feedback loops are intuitive and lead to easy to implement corrective actions, both of which gives the evaluation high utility.

When I first began evaluating feedback loops, I felt evaluators needed some standard against which to judge feedback *quality*. McShane and Von Glinow (2009) identify five criteria for useful feedback: credibility, relevance, timeliness, frequency, and specificity. In my experience, however, the criterion that supersedes these is to first ascertain whether the feedback loop is closed. If the feedback isn't received, then evaluating its quality is moot.

Closing the Loop: Feedback Needs to Be Received Before It Can Be Acted Upon

In evaluating my county's pandemic response, I looked for places where information was being exchanged, because in a time-urgent event like a pandemic response, delayed feedback has direct and immediate consequences for saving lives. An easily defined emergency response subsystem is an emergency operating center (EOC). An EOC is the response coordination control center and its boundaries are easily demarcated by the physical building in which it resides. Within the EOC there are many system actors who are organized into an incident command system (ICS). There are hundreds of information exchanges within an ICS daily, if not hourly.

EOC information exchanges are dependent on completing and sending numerous electronic forms (Emergency Management Institute, n.d.). I observed that the logistics chief (i.e., responsible for moving supplies) was becoming increasingly frustrated because the incident commander had not "replied" to a request made on ICS Form 213, requesting instruction where to ship required personal protection equipment (PPE). The consequence of failing to close this feedback loop was that PPE desperately needed by frontline health care workers sat idle in a warehouse. My evaluation recommendation was to remind the incident commander to create a simple rule to close all Form 213 requests within 24 hours.

GENERAL MESSAGE (ICS 213)

| 1. Incident Name (Optional): |
| 2. To (Name and Position): |
| 3. From (Name and Position): |
| 4. Subject: | 5. Date: | 6. Time |
| 7. Message: |
| 8. Approved by: Name ___ Signature: ___ Position/Title ___ |
| 9. Reply: |
| 10. Replied by: Name ___ Position/Title: ___ Signature: ___ |
| ICS 213 | Date/Time: |

Figure 7.1   Pima County EOC. *Photo Credit:* Pima County.

Other Real-World Applications.   Successful outcomes in a cardiac event depend on getting a patient as quickly as possible to a definitive care facility. In rural areas, many community hospitals are not staffed nor equipped for dealing with cardiac events. During the full-scale exercises (Chapter 5), I observed firsthand that too often patients were being transported to the nearest community hospital, only to have to be transported again to a hospital that could support the patient's needs. In a situation where minutes make the difference between life and death, most patients do not survive this logistical error.

The solution was for medics on scene to send an EKG to the nearest community hospital. The attending physician would then read the EKG, recognize it is a cardiac event, and reroute the ambulance directly to the definitive care facility.

The EKG transmission-hospital feedback loop depended on two system attributes: training and functional information systems (Chapter 4). My evaluation confirmed that all medics had completed the necessary training. The problem was an unreliable information system infrastructure. Connectivity in rural areas is sporadic, so the EKG was often "stuck" in the transmission mode; the loop was not being closed. To solve this problem, we mapped out points of connectivity in every rural road in the county and calculated the fastest routes to the nearest point of connectivity (i.e., where the loop could be closed) that did not limit the hospital choice of the ambulance (Harness et al., 2019).

As these examples illustrate, closing the loop is critical for system success, once you have established that feedback loops are being closed, then you can begin evaluating the extent to which the other feedback criteria are being met.

Credibility: The Feedback Recipient Must Deem the Information To Be Credible or It Will Not Be Used for Decision-Making

The disastrous consequences when feedback is not deemed credible is well illustrated by the conflicting messaging between those with a political agenda and public health agencies (Carter & May, 2020; Piller, 2020). In the pandemic, conflicting messaging by politicians undermined the credibility of the public health institutions at all system levels (federal, state, local). It is this reality that was arguably the greatest contributing factor to face-covering noncompliance and vaccination refusal, two mitigation and prevention strategies that could have conservatively saved an estimated 100,000 U.S. lives (Gakidou, 2020).

When the credibility of the feedback is brought into question it can have dire consequences.

Other Real-World Applications. Centers for translational cancer research (CTR) focus on supporting investigators in moving cancer research from the laboratory into clinical practice and the community. Through stakeholder interviews, our evaluation team learned that some CTR team members perceived other CTR team members as less credible because they didn't possess what they considered to be necessary credentials, in this case an MD. Thus, the advice of these team members was less likely to be adopted. This, in turn, introduced inefficiencies that reduced the likelihood of the CTR being able to fulfill its mandate. This finding was similar to problems noted by researchers studying the development of interprofessional teams (Carlisle et al., 2004).

As these examples illustrate, there are many factors influencing feedback credibility (e.g., status, degree, trust). If the feedback is not deemed credible, then the system may not respond as intended/needed, that is, the system becomes inefficient.

Relevance: If Feedback Lacks Relevance, Then the Intended Target Cannot Use the Information to Assist Decision-Making

Early in the pandemic there was considerable variation in community transmission by geographic location. The Centers for Disease Control (CDC) provided community transmission data at the zip code and census tract levels allowing local jurisdictions to tailor and customize their responses (Arizona Department of Health Services, n.d.; Centers for Disease Control and Prevention, n.d.). States who chose to use this information had significantly less deaths per 100,000 than states who chose to ignore the science (Austin, 2020).

Other Real-World Applications. I spent over 25 years as a professor, teaching evaluation. I often created group assignments in the interest of building students' skills in group reflection and feedback processes. I made the assumption that students would be able to gauge their peers' work effectively, however, this was rarely the case. Many peers were able to provide accurate feedback, for example on how to improve wording of a sentence, but too often were unable to provide relevant feedback; that is, feedback specific to the content of the assignment (Chong, 2017). The peer feedback did not play out as intended and there were plenty of hurt feelings. Even worse was that the student assignments were way off base because the irrelevant feedback sent them caroming in the wrong direction. I thought the group assignment was going to be efficient and enhance student skill sets, but it ended up costing us all more time and grief!

These examples reinforce the need for the feedback to be judged as relevant for system actors to act on the information. If not deemed relevant, then the feedback needed to maintain or improve system efficiency will be ignored.

Timeliness: Feedback That Comes Too Soon or Too Late May Not Be Useful to Improve System Efficiency

One recurring problem throughout the pandemic was the time delay in getting test results. Often people waited for more than a week to receive their test results. Since many people treated the COVID-19 test more like a cholesterol test (i.e., the results of which do not impact others) they did not stay home and quarantine (Lin-Fischer, 2020). The failure to provide timely feedback about test results meant many people who were COVID-19 positive did not stay at home and thus the disease continued to be spread.

Other Real-World Applications. In evaluating pool safety, I learned by observing inspectors in their daily routine that the policy was for pools to be tested twice a day for chlorine and PH levels (Figure 7.2). However, the timing of those measurements was not specified. An inspection of the pool logs found that operators were abusing this loophole. For example, some operators would test the same pool just 5 minutes apart! They were in compliance, but the second measurement defeated the quality control purpose. The policy was subsequently changed to better specify the timing between measurements.

These examples highlight the importance of feedback timing. Feedback coming too soon may be judged to be irrelevant, while feedback coming too late may no longer be useful in making system adjustments to improve efficiency.

Frequency: The Rate at Which Feedback Is Provided Can Be Critically Important

The pandemic was a rapidly evolving event, so the frequency at which feedback was forthcoming was critical in mounting an appropriate response. To meet this need, the CDC made available near-real time data updates to the case count, hospitalization rates, and deaths by census tract and zip code. This near-real time feedback was essential

Figure 7.2 Testing pool PH (left) and verifying pool records (right).

for emergency management, helping anticipate how to reallocate resources in anticipation of case surges.

Other Real-World Applications. One grocery store I was evaluating for COVID-19 compliance was having challenges reminding customers about the face covering mandate. Customers flow in and out of a grocery store throughout the day. As the store manager noted during my interview with him, "We don't have the money to pay someone to be the mask police." The solution was to use the public address system to politely remind customers of the mandate. To determine the frequency of the announcements the store used data on their customer throughput. Based on these data, public address announcements were scheduled every 20 minutes to maximize the likelihood of getting the message to as many new customers as possible, without annoying those who were already in the store with repeated messages.

One key to successful feedback is the pace or schedule at which it is provided. When feedback is fast and furious, it may overwhelm system actors and thus be ignored. On the other hand, when feedback does not come at the intervals needed it may cause the system to slow down as it waits for information needed to guide ongoing corrections.

Specificity

The more specific the feedback, the clearer what needs to be done becomes, and the more likely it is to be used to make decisions. If the feedback contains too much information, then the recipient is less likely to filter the important information from the "noise"

In the pandemic, "nonspecific" feedback public messaging created many cascading problems. For example, using the phrase "social distancing" led to social isolation and degraded mental health. The problem was that the term social distancing is nonspecific, being used to refer to the "physical distancing" requirements for reducing disease spread. It is certainly possible to maintain social closeness while remaining physically distant, but many suffered unintended mental health problems because of the literal interpretation of the term social distancing (Aminnejad & Alikhani, 2020; Freedman, 2020).

Other Real-World Applications. In my evaluation of a food safety system, I shadowed health inspectors and observed that several restaurant operators failed to implement the inspectors' feedback needed to keep their food establishments in compliance. Through operator interviews I learned that the corrective actions being recommended by some of the inspectors did not contain sufficient detail for the operator to act. For example, cleaning dishes is a three-step process: wash–rinse–sanitize.

The chemical mixture in the sanitizing process is critical: too little and the dishes may still contain harmful germs that can spread food borne illness, too much and the chemical residue can harm people. The correct mixture is evaluated using a chemical test strip. Some inspectors would simply show the operator the results of the chemical test strip and ask them to correct the problem. Many operators did not know how to get the correct sanitizing mixture. Afterall, parts per million (ppm) is a difficult thing to visualize. Those inspectors, who provided more specific feedback, for example by showing the operator how to mark the sink with the correct amount of hot water for a given amount of chemical, had better compliance rates.

When feedback is nonspecific it may add to the system "noise" making it difficult for the system actors to filter what is usable. This may cause the wrong information to be acted upon and/or the correct information to be ignored. In either case, system inefficiency is introduced.

Feedback Loops to Improve Program Theory

Recall in Chapter 1, I used an obesity example to illustrate how limitations with the logic model gave rise to systems thinking. One of the limitations I noted was that a program's theory is usually represented as a series of linear relationships between underlying conditions; a result of mirroring the reductionist research upon which it is predicated.

To illustrate how a feedback loop can create a better, more realistic, and common sense understanding of a program theory, consider the example in Figure 7.3. Here, the program logic is that low self-esteem leads to a sedentary lifestyle, which in turn contributes to obesity. An intervention based on this set of program assumptions might be some type of psychological intervention to improve self-esteem.

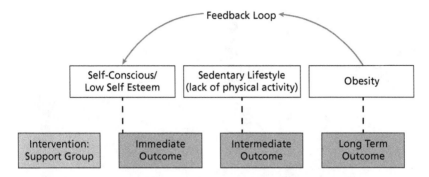

Figure 7.3 An example of augmenting program theory by applying the feedback loop systems thinking principle.

However, in reality, the relationship between the three conditions in Figure 7.3 is more sophisticated, nonlinear, and cyclical. The research shows that increases in obesity are known to negatively influence self-esteem, low self-esteem negatively influences physical activity, and a lack of physical activity positively influences obesity (which is not a good thing). This relationship between these underlying conditions can be better depicted by placing a feedback loop linking obesity back to self-esteem.

If the conditions underlying obesity are related circularly, then by definition different interventions could be introduced at different points in the cycle. This is in fact the reality as evidenced by interventions designed to address self-esteem (e.g., family and peer support groups), sedentary lifestyle (e.g., making access to physical activity easier), and obesity (e.g., bariatric surgery). This understanding also renders the notion of delineating outcomes as being immediate, intermediate, and long-term (as the logic model does) moot. They are all simply outcomes in the cycle needing to be evaluated.

Feedback Loops: Something to Ponder

From these examples I hope you agree that the feedback loop can be a powerful system principle in evaluation. It is my experience that recommendations related to improving feedback loops are almost always adopted by decision-makers. I believe this to be the case because the deficiency is usually easy to understand and correct. However, I worry about the tendency to get carried away with feedback loops and overly large diagrams. For example, several articles were published using

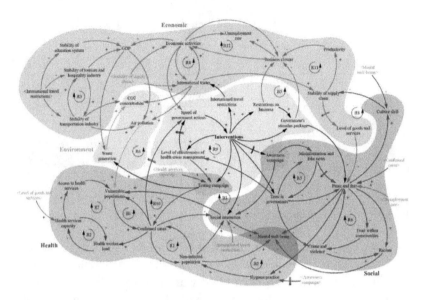

Figure 7.4 A casual loop analysis of the COVID-19 pandemic (Sahin et al., 2020).

causal loop diagrams to explain the pandemic (e.g., Sahin et al., 2020; Sy et al., 2020). Causal loop diagrams are essentially a "collection of feedback loops" that are used to explain how a system operates. One such causal loop diagram is shown in Figure 7.4.

I understand the science of causal loop diagrams like that shown in Figure 7.4 and I understand the work is intended to make sense to those who were involved in creating it. There are even some examples of systems whose foundations, appropriately so, rest entirely on the feedback loop principle, like the health information exchange systems I evaluated (Kuperman, 2011). However, from an evaluation practice-based perspective, the majority of causal loop diagram work I have encountered tends to be purely an "academic" exercise, in every pejorative sense of the term without a clear pathway forward towards action or change (Checkland, 2000). There are some useful and effective exceptions using causal loop diagrams, such as the work of Allender and colleagues whereby whole communities using these types of models are empowered to understand their unique system and create change through multiple actions occurring simultaneously across a system (Allender et al., 2015).

Cascading Failures

A cascading failure is a process in a system comprising intercon-nected parts in which the failure of one or a few parts can trigger the failure of other parts ("Cascading Failure," 2022). It is essentially a downstream domino effect created by upstream dependencies (Renger et al., 2017). Some have termed this a "knock-on" effect. The cascading failure principle is another way of understanding interdependencies.

In the pandemic, there was much discussion about the need to "flatten the curve" (Figure 7.5). Flattening the curve was based on an understanding of the cascading failures principle. Early on, health of-ficials recognized the interdependency between community transmis-sion rate and hospital capacity. To prevent downstream hospital ca-pacity problems, public health officials called on a host of mitigation strategies to slow the disease spread, such as stay-at-home orders, mask-ing, bar and gym closures, and so forth.

The flattening the curve example illustrates the predictive power of the cascading failures principle. By defining where interdependen-cies exist, one is able to project where a problem may occur and appro-priately focus evaluation resources. In my experience we seldom do this type of evaluation. Our evaluation training and methods are geared to understanding why problems occur after they present themselves.

The cascading failures principle also has explanatory power. For ex-ample, an important part of the pandemic response was vaccination dis-tribution. One common way of delivering mass vaccinations is through the use of points of dispensing (POD). A POD is a complex intervention acting as a system that consists of many parts, called stations, contribut-ing to the goal of maximizing throughput. The stations are purposively

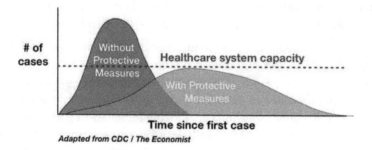

Adapted from CDC / The Economist

Figure 7.5 Flattening the curve requires an implicit understanding of down-stream dependencies. *Source:* Roberts, 2020.

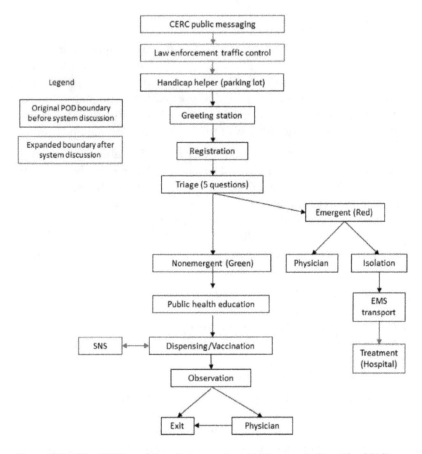

Figure 7.6 The POD workflow being evaluated (Renger & Granillo, 2018).

sequenced beginning with registration, then eligibility, then education, then the vaccination, and finally observation before being released. The workflow for the POD exercise I evaluated is shown in Figure 7.6.

I observed that the POD was not meeting its throughput goal. During the exercise, the registration station was getting backed up, overwhelmed by a patient surge. The incident commander was focused on solving the problem at the station where the back-up was occurring. While that is a good place to begin looking for an answer, the cascading failures principle helped me understand that the source of the problem was actually occurring elsewhere. In this case the surge at the registration station was caused by upstream issues related to poor public messaging and lapses in traffic control (Renger & Granillo, 2018). Interestingly both of these upstream causes fell outside the initial system boundaries demarcated for evaluation purposes! This serves as an important reminder that evaluation findings may cause you to redefine your system boundaries (Chapter 6).

Lorenz (1979) observed that the tiniest alteration in starting conditions could result in radically different weather forecasts. He called this a "butterfly effect" because he argued that a flap of a butterfly wing could, in theory, be the event that changes the weather trajectory to create a tornado. This is a nuanced form of a domino effect, where an upstream event doesn't necessarily result in cascading failures, but triggers a different trajectory of cascading events.

Other Real-World Applications. Earlier in the chapter I noted the life and death consequences of the failure to close a feedback loop in a cardiac event. I'll now explain how I was able to find the source of the problem by applying the cascading failure principle.

As you learned in Chapter 5, I tested SET using full-scale exercises. To evaluate these exercises, I located trained evaluators at each exchange point in the cardiac care system (see Figure 7.7). As the evaluator at the heart hospital, I observed that the staff hadn't been preparing for the

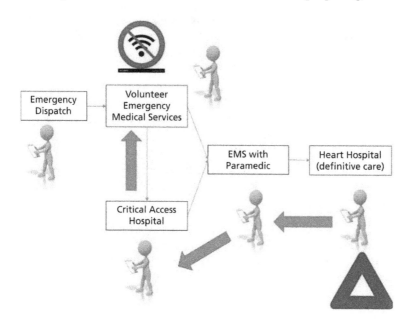

Figure 7.7 Positioning evaluators at different parts of the cardiac care system response.

arrival of the patient as per the SOP. I called the first upstream evaluator, who noted that the paramedic was also in standby mode waiting for instruction from the critical access hospital. Something was very wrong. I kept moving upstream until I reached the evaluator working with the volunteer ambulance service. There I learned that the ambulance staff were still trying to acquire a Wi-Fi signal to send the EKG. The failure to close that loop had a downstream domino effect on the coordination of the entire response system.

Reflex Arc

A reflex arc is the human body's mechanism for responding more efficiently to a stimulus by bypassing the need to send the signal to the brain for processing (Dewey, 1896). For example, the reflex arc helps you pull your hand away from the hot stove before you feel the pain.

The reflex arc is one of the more difficult to understand, yet potentially the most powerful system principle in evaluation practice. It is more challenging to understand because the application from biological to complex interventions acting as systems seems abstract. From a practice standpoint a reflex arc is simply a bypass intended to improve efficiency.

An example of a reflex arc in the pandemic was the implementation of standing, do-not-resuscitate (DNR) orders. Normally, as part of the hospital SOPs, physicians must sign off on all orders. A physician signature is necessary for quality patient care and to safeguard against liability. However, it can often take days or weeks for busy clinicians to work through the paperwork and sign off (Neimanis et al., 2017). In the pandemic, the hospitals were overwhelmed, understaffed, and under equipped. Waiting for a signature to terminate life of someone whose condition was irreversible, meant that access to that lifesaving equipment was being withheld from those who could possibly benefit (Masson, 2020). The DNR order was considered as a bypass to save time and resources.

In my experience, the reflex arc is very useful in offering recommendations to improve system efficiency. Evaluation branches devoted to continuous quality improvement ([CQI]; see below) could especially benefit from applying this system's principle.

Other Real-World Applications. Participants in my Mall of America system evaluation workshop (Chapter 3) noticed restaurants using two reflex arcs to improve efficiency. The first was a cash register that included single keys for common denominations of cash tendered, such as $5, $10, and $20 bills. For example, it would normally take five keystrokes to enter a $20.00 cash tender, one "2," three "0s," and the decimal. With the help of an information systems bypass this was reduced to a single key.

The second example was the self-serve soda refill machine. Allowing customers to get their own refills bypassed the need for a staff to attend to the customer request. This increased the efficiency on two fronts. First, from the customer perspective there was no waiting; they were able to get exactly what they wanted, when they wanted. Second, from the staff perspective, they were able to devote their full attention to new customers, ensuring their orders are correctly filled more quickly. Both these efficiencies increased the likelihood of having satisfied customers, the emergent system property!

A third example of using a reflex arc to improve efficiency comes from my experience in managing my own evaluation team. In the cardiac care system evaluation, I was responsible for coordinating an evaluation team of 10. The university protocol, aka the SOP, was that I needed to sign off on all grant-related purchases. This was horribly inefficient: it was costing about 2 hours of staff time, which meant well over $100 to approve a $5.00 stapler. To improve our team efficiency, I instituted a simple rule that acted as a bypass, giving all team members the power to purchase anything under $1,000 without needing to have a discussion with me first.

Reflex Arcs: A Word of Warning

As noted earlier, system inefficiencies are discovered by comparing the observed process to the stated process (i.e., the SOP). However, it would be a mistake to always assume that observed departures from the stated SOP are inefficiencies. In fact, the observed departure from the stated SOP might be an organically derived bypass to *improve* efficiency. Margaret Wheatley put it this way: "Somewhere in the system are people already practicing a solution that others think is impossible. Or they possess information that could help many others. Or they defy stereotypes and have the very capabilities we need" (Barlow & Stone, 2011, p. 5). For example, sometimes staff at the operational level encounter implementation challenges for which they develop their own workaround. That workaround, in my experience, is almost always a reflex arc. The new process is an efficiency, but hasn't been documented in the SOPs.

The disconnect between what is written and what is happening on the ground occurs quite often. Burnes (2005) described it this way:

> Emergent change occurs when people reaccomplish routines and when they deal with contingencies, breakdowns, and opportunities in everyday work. Much of this change goes unnoticed, because small alternations are lumped together as noise in otherwise uneventful inertia. (p. 75)

There are many reasons for this disconnect including the failure of the evaluator to get the perspectives of system actors at the operational level when defining the system (i.e., Step 5, defining the system), or it may be an underlying culture issue being expressed as a lack of diligence or commitment to update and/or maintain accurate written SOPs.

On the other hand, sometimes the observed bypass is simply a training failure (Chapter 4) where the system actor does not understand how to execute the SOP. For example, in the pandemic response, public health officials assumed many of the roles in the ICS. The problem is that public health officials have little practical experience operating as an ICS. This meant public health personnel often, incorrectly, bypassed the chain of command, causing major delays as people had to retrace their steps and go through the appropriate channels. The evaluation showed that the bypass was due to a lack of training, and this created confusion and system waste; system waste being defined as unnecessarily repeating process steps (Kilpatrick, 2003).

Evaluating System Efficiency: Learning From the CQI Literature

CQI is, by definition, devoted to improving efficiencies. A significant body of the CQI literature, like six sigma, is devoted to advancing methods for improving processes in organizations and service industries (Antony, 2006; Kumar et al., 2013). Organizations are of course systems, so I am always looking to the CQI literature for methods to augment my evaluation of system efficiency.

Two especially useful and interdependent CQI concepts, introduced to me by my good friend Brian Keogh, are reworks and system waste. Reworks occur when a system process is duplicated. Sometimes system redundancies are necessary, especially when issues of safety are concerned. On the other hand, reworks are wasteful, or inefficient, when the duplication is unnecessary. For example, in the cardiac care system I noted the hospital and ambulance service completing the same steps, simultaneously! Both agencies assumed they were responsible for securing a nurse practitioner (i.e., who had authority to administer drugs) for transport to a definitive care facility. This was causing mass confusion. When I discovered this unnecessary duplication I brought both groups together in a tabletop style exercise (Chapter 6). By talking through a scenario requiring transport to a definitive care facility they were able to discover for themselves what I had learned. They then modified their SOPs so that only one agency assumed the responsibility going forward.

Another example of unnecessary duplication is from an evaluation I completed with pool safety inspectors. Inspectors need to document whether the appropriate safety signage is posted for all pools and spas. The inspectors I shadowed were completing a safety compliance form for each pool/spa. I observed, however, that often there were several pools or spas in the same enclosure. To my systems way of thinking the enclosure defined the system boundaries that included several parts (pools and spas). By county law the signage for all pools and spas within the same enclosure must be posted at the entrance gate and/or on the enclosure (i.e., the perimeter fence) itself. In other words, only one sign was needed to cover all the pools and spas in the enclosure, yet reports were needed for each separate pool and spa. My recommendation to complete a single form for all pools and spas within the same enclosure was adopted within a week and is saving numerous inspectors several hours each month. This meant more time could be devoted to doing additional inspections, thus ensuring more of the public was safe.

As I alluded to above, not all reworks are unnecessary duplications. For example, when evaluating the Snakes & Latte coffeehouse, I asked the owner, Aaron, why his SOP requires that a customer's order be repeated aloud all down the line. He noted that this was purposeful to safeguard against customers with a peanut allergy.

Hospital SOPs also build in numerous, necessary redundancies. For example, during my colonoscopy procedure I was asked for my name and date of birth at each system handoff (registration, gastroenterology intake, nurse, anesthesiologist, attendant, and the doctor). In a high-volume environment like a hospital these redundancies are necessary safeguards against wrong site, wrong procedure, and wrong patient mistakes (Michaels et al., 2007).

Conclusion

Evaluating system efficiency is tantamount to evaluating the interdependencies between system parts. This chapter highlighted three system principles that I found particularly useful in my evaluation practice to identify and evaluate the interdependencies of complex interventions acting as a system. There are many other system principles whose potential for evaluating interdependencies have yet to be uncovered. Recall from Chapter 5 that SET (Renger, 2015) recognizes this reality and is purposively designed to accommodate the inclusion of additional systems principles. In the next chapter I use a family case study to help reinforce the understanding of these system principles for evaluating interdependencies and the importance of their methodical application.

References

Allender, S., Owen, B., Kuhlberg, J., Lowe, J., Nagorcka-Smith, P., Whelan, J., & Bell, C. (2015). A community based systems diagram of obesity causes. *PLOS ONE, 10*(7), e0129683. https://doi.org/10.1371/journal .pone.0129683

Aminnejad, R., & Alikhani, R. (2020). Physical distancing or social distancing: That is the question. *Canadian Journal of Anesthesiology, 67,* 1457–1458. https://doi.org/10.1007/s12630-020-01697-2

Antony, J. (2006). Six sigma for service processes. *Business Process Management Journal, 12*(2), 234–248. https://doi.org/10.1108/14637150610657558

Arizona Department of Health Services. (n.d.). *Highlighted infectious diseases for Arizona.* https://www.azdhs.gov/preparedness/epidemiology-disease-control/infectious-disease-epidemiology/index.php#novel-coronavirus-home

Austin, A. (2020, August 11). *Red states far worse than blue for current Covid-19 deaths. Not even close.* Daily Kos. https://www.dailykos.com/stories/2020/8/11/1968337/-Red-states-far-worse-than-blue-for-current-Covid-19-deaths-Not-even-close

Barlow, Z., & Stone, M. K. (2011). Living systems and leadership: Cultivating conditions for institutional change. *Journal of Sustainability Education, 2*(1), 1–29.

Burnes, B. (2005). Complexity theory and organizational change. *International Journal of Management Reviews, 7*(2), 73–90. https://doi.org/10.1111/j.1468-2370.2005.00107.x

Carlisle, C., Cooper, H., & Watkins, C. (2004). "Do none of you talk to each other?" The challenges facing the implementation of interprofessional education. *Medical Teacher, 26*(6), 545–552. https://doi.org/10.1080/61421590410001711616

Carter, D. P., & May, P. J. (2020). Making sense of the US COVID-19 pandemic response: A policy regime perspective. *Administrative Theory & Praxis, 42*(2), 265–277. https://doi.org/10.1080/10841806.2020.1758991

Cascading Failure. (2022, August 6). In *Wikipedia.* https://en.wikipedia.org/wiki/Cascading_failure

Centers for Disease Control and Prevention. (n.d.). *United States COVID-19 cases, deaths, and laboratory testing (NAATs) by state, territory, and jurisdiction.* https://www.cdc.gov/coronavirus/2019-ncov/cases-updates/cases-in-us.html

Checkland, P. (2000). Soft systems methodology: A thirty-year retrospective. *Systems Research and Behavioral Science, 17,* 11–58. https://doi.org/10.1002/1099-1743(200011)17:1+<::AID-SRES374>3.0.CO;2-O

Chong, I. (2017). How students' ability levels influence the relevance and accuracy of feedback to their peers: A case study. *Assessing Writing, 31,* 13–23. https://doi.org/10.1016/j.asw.2016.07.002

Deming, W. E. (n.d.). *Quote: Every system is perfectly designed to get the results it gets.* https://deming.org/quotes/10141/

Dewey, J. (1896). The reflex arc concept in psychology. *Psychological Review, 3*(4), 357–370. https://doi.org/10.1037/h0070405

Emergency Management Institute. (n.d.). *ICS fillable forms.* https://training
.fema.gov/icsresource/icsforms.aspx

Freedman, W. (2020, December 7). *Bay area workers in 'gray area' confused
over CA's new shelter in place rules.* ABC News. https://abc7news.com/
coronavirus-marin-county-california-stay-at-home-order-shelter-in-place
-update/8594099/

Gakidou, E. (2020). *Global projections of potential lives saved from COVID-19
through universal mask use.* The IHME COVID-19 Forecasting Team.
https://doi.org/10.1101/2020.10.08.20209510

Gear, C., Eppel, E., & Koziol-Mclain, J. (2018). Advancing complexity
theory as a qualitative research methodology. *International Journal of
Qualitative Methods, 17*(1), 1609406918782557. https://doi.org/10
.1177/1609406918782557

Haines, S. G. (2000). *The systems thinking approach to strategic planning and
management.* St. Lucie Press.

Harness, D., Sullivan, S., Keegan, J., Taylor, C., Neibauer, T., Jones, I., Pratt,
K., Odenbach, H., Schueler, M., Renger, J., Renger, J., & Renger, R.
(2019, September 3). Coordinating a ground-air intercept: Lessons
learned. *Journal of Emergency Medical Services.* https://www.jems.com/
administration-and-leadership/coordinating-a-ground-air-intercept
-lessons-learned/

Ison, R. L. (2008). Systems thinking and practice for action research. In
P. W. Reason & H. Bradbury (Eds.), *The SAGE handbook of action re-
search participative inquiry and practice* (2nd ed., pp. 139–158.). SAGE
Publications.

Jackson, B. A., Faith, K. S., & Willis, H. H. (2012). Evaluating the reliability of
emergency response systems for large-scale incident operations. *Rand
Health Quarterly, 2*(3), 8. https://www.rand.org/pubs/periodicals/
health-quarterly/issues/v2/n3/08.html

Kilpatrick, J. (2003). Lean principles. *Utah Manufacturing Extension Partnership, 68*, 1–5.

Kumar, S., Satsangi, P. S., & Prajapati, D. R. (2013). Improvement of Sigma level of a foundry: A case study. *The TQM Journal, 25*(1), 29–43.
https://doi.org/10.1108/17542731311286414

Kuperman, G. J. (2011). Health-information exchange: Why are we doing
it, and what are we doing? *Journal of the American Medical Informatics Association, 18*(5), 678–682. https://doi.org/10.1136/amiajnl-2010-00
0021

Lin-Fischer, B. (2020). *Waiting for coronavirus test results? Self-quarantine while
you wait, official says.* MSN.

Lorenz, E. (1979). *Predictability: Does the flap of a butterfly's wing in Brazil set
off a tornado in Texas?* Address at the American Association for the
Advancement of Science, Washington, DC.

Masson, G. (2020, March 25). "We're going to be coding dead people": Hospitals consider do-not-resuscitate order for all COVID-19 patients. *Becker's Hospital Review.* https://www.beckershospitalreview.com/public-health/we-re-going-to-be-coding-dead-people-hospitals-consider-do-not-resuscitate-order-for-all-covid-19-patients.html

Mcshane, S., & Von Glinow, M. (2009). *Organizational behavior: Emerging knowledge and practice for the real world* (5th ed.). McGraw Hill.

Michaels, R. K., Makary, M. A., Dahab, Y., Frassica, F. J., Heitmiller, E., Rowen, L. C., Crotreau, R., Brem, H., & Pronovost, P. J. (2007). Achieving the National Quality Forum's "Never Events": Prevention of wrong site, wrong procedure, and wrong patient operations. *Annals of surgery, 245*(4), 526–532. https://doi.org/10.1097/01.sla.0000251573.52463.d2

Neimanis, I., Gaebel, K., Dickson, R., Levy, R., Goebel, C., Zizzo, A., Woods, A., & Corsini, J. (2017). Referral processes and physician wait times. *Canadian Family Physician, 63*(8), 619–624.

Piller, C. (2020). Undermining CDC. *Science, 370*(6515), 394–399. http://doi.org/10.1126/science.370.6515.394

Renger, R. (2015). System evaluation theory (SET). *Evaluation Journal of Australasia, 15*(4), 16–28. https://doi.org/10.1177/1035719X1501500403

Renger, R. (2016). Illustrating the evaluation of system feedback mechanisms using system evaluation theory (SET). *Evaluation Journal of Australasia, 16*(4), 15–21. https://doi.org/10.1177/1035719X1601600403

Renger, R. (2021). COVID-19: Exposing the need for emergency management to invest in systems thinking. *Journal of Emergency Management (Weston, Mass.), 19*(7), 39–48. https://doi.org/10.5055/jem.0607

Renger, R., Foltysova, J., Ienuso, S., Renger, J., & Booze, W. (2017). Evaluating system cascading failures. *Evaluation Journal of Australasia, 17*(2), 29–36. https://doi.org/10.1177/1035719X1701700205

Renger, R., & Granillo, B. (2018). Using systems evaluation theory (SET) to improve points of dispensing (POD) planning, training, and evaluation. *Journal of Emergency Management, 16*(3), 149–157. https://doi.org/10.5055/jem.2018.0364

Renger, R., Renger, J., Van Eck, R. N., Basson, M. D., & Renger, J. (2022). A call for evaluation utility metrics (EUMs). *Canadian Journal of Program Evaluation, 37*(1). https://doi.org/10.3138/cjpe.72386

Roberts, S. (2020, March 27). Flattening the Coronavirus curve. *The New York Times.* https://www.nytimes.com/article/flatten-curve-coronavirus.html

Sahin, O., Salim, H., Suprun, E., Richards, R., MacAskill, S., Heilgeist, S., Rutherford, S., Stewart, R. A., & Beal, C. D. (2020). Developing a preliminary causal loop diagram for understanding the wicked complexity of the COVID-19 pandemic. *Systems, 8(2),* 20. https://doi.org/10.3390/systems8020020

Sy, C., Bernardo, E., Miguel, A., San Juan, J. L., Mayol, A. P., Ching, P. M., Culaba, A. Ubando, A., & Mutuc, J. E. (2020). Policy development for pandemic response using system dynamics: A case study on COVID-19. *Process Integration and Optimization for Sustainability, 4,* 497–501. https://doi.org/10.1007/s41660-020-00130-x

8

Evaluating System Interdependencies Using a Family System Case Example

And you think your family has problems...

In this chapter I illustrate how to apply the system principles to which you've been introduced thus far to define a family system and evaluate its interdependencies. I deliberately sought an example that could be relatable to all readers, one that does not require any specific area of substantive expertise. Even though families come in all shapes and sizes the blueprint for applying system principles to evaluate system efficiency is the same regardless of the complexity (i.e., family members and interdependencies).

Family System Case Example

Imagine that I am approached by the parents of the three-person family asking for help to resolve a family challenge. I agree to meet them

System Evaluation Theory, pages 141–158
Copyright © 2022 by Information Age Publishing
www.infoagepub.com

to talk through the issue. In my initial meeting with the parents, I pay close attention to their language. In describing their challenges, they use phrases like, "Our child isn't cooperating" and "We seem to stumble over each other each morning." These phrases serve as indicators to me of system parts not working together; issues of interdependence. They also use phrases like, "The three of us just don't seem to be on the same page" and "We don't seem to share the same family values." These phrases signal the family is trying to accomplish some type of higher purpose; indicators of emergence. I conclude after this meeting that I am dealing with more than just "a bunch of stuff" (Meadows, 2008) and that evaluating the family as a system is appropriate because all family members are interconnected, and together the family unit has the goals to learn, grow, love, and to live in harmony.

I am also comforted that the environment is fertile ground for conducting the evaluation. Afterall, the parents, the family leaders, came to me for help, are engaged, and motivated to make their family system better. In short, my system evaluation readiness scan (SERS) resulted in a thumbs up.

SET Step 1: Defining the Complex Family Acting as a System

My next meeting with the family focuses on understanding the emergent system property, that is what the family means by "getting on the same page." The family notes that when all the family members (i.e., the system parts) are working together they would hope to achieve family harmony.

I then work with the parents to define the system parts key to enabling harmony to emerge. The parents initially include themselves and their child. Together we connect the arrows between the three family members to create our initial family boundary. I try pushing the boundary envelope by asking whether extended family members or close family friends should be included, but the family says no because they want to focus on those living under their roof.

As my discussion with the parents continues, I learn they are especially frustrated with their family routine: Too many opportunities for shared meals are being missed, especially breakfast. They would like an opportunity to discuss, as a family, what each person will be doing that day and offer encouragement to each other. They know the importance that sharing a meal together has on building feelings of togetherness and harmony ("Make Mealtime Family Time," n.d.), but can't seem to get coordinated to make this happen.

Because of the focus on breakfast, we further narrow the boundaries to their morning routine, from the time they wake up (7:00 a.m.) to when they would share breakfast together (8:00 a.m.). I now recognize I'm working at an even smaller system level. Building from my own experience I know I am dependent on setting my phone's alarm to wake me up, on the coffee machine working, the shower having hot water, and so forth. So, I again challenge the boundary envelope by asking the extent to which the family's information systems infrastructure plays a role in the coordination. The parents then explain that their morning routines depend on many different types of technology. I then include these as system parts and revisit the exercise of connecting them using arrows to the family members.

I then proceed to unpack the arrows. I first meet individually with each family member to define their *individual* system operating procedures ([SOP]; i.e., their routines) using process flow mapping (Renger et al., 2016). I then meet with all three family members and develop the *joint* SOP ([JSOP]; see Figure 8.1). In Figure 8.1, time is depicted on the left-hand side. To reduce clutter, I do not depict each minute on the timeline; you can assume the 60 minutes are spaced at regular intervals.

SET Step 2: Evaluating Family System Efficiency (i.e., Interdependencies)

Before investing in costly data collection, I conduct a cursory analysis of the JSOP so I can better anticipate where to target my evaluation efforts. My analysis consists of looking where information is exchanged (i.e., feedback loops), possible processes that can lead to a domino

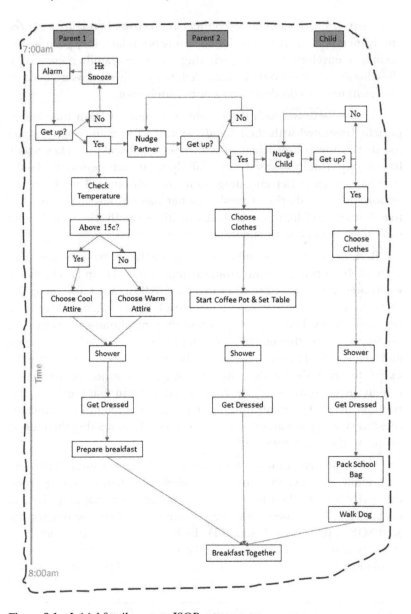

Figure 8.1 Initial family system JSOP.

effect of problems (i.e., cascading failure), and places where efficiencies might be achieved by creating a bypass (i.e., reflex arc)

There is no particular order in which I consider the three system principles of evaluating system efficiency, but I methodically apply them all. In this instance, I begin by applying the cascading failures principle only because there was an obvious choke point as I scanned the JSOP (Renger et al., 2017).

When I first began my systems thinking journey, nothing in a SOP really stood out to me, they just looked complex. However, as you gain experience with mapping SOPs and applying system principles you too will be able to identify major issues. In fact, I promise you that with experience you will begin to identify system efficiency issues *during* the SOP mapping process! My experience is when system actors are alerted to these potential problems, they make immediate SOP refinements. Yarbrough (2017) notes that this kind of stakeholder action is an indicator of evaluation utility! Thus, the mere facilitation of the mapping process leads to an improved SOP (Renger et al., 2021).

From the cascading failures principle, I know that a problem occurring with one family member's routine can have downstream consequences for that person as well as other family members. Looking at the JSOP, it is immediately evident that all three family members intend to shower at the same time. Of course, that's not an issue if there are three showers and ample hot water, but context is important. Having visited with the family in their home, I know there is only one shower and each family member would like privacy when they shower. Thus, under the existing SOP, if Parent 1 takes a 10-min shower, then this will delay Parent 2 by 10 minutes. If Parent 2 takes a 15-minute shower their child is delayed by 25 minutes. This would make it impossible for Parent 2 and the child to make breakfast on time. The cascading effect is illustrated in Figure 8.2. The boxes with a yield sign symbol next to them denote a warning that processes are being delayed. The boxes with a stop sign symbol next to them signify that the processes will extend beyond the established time boundary.

One solution to this problem is for the family members to restructure their processes so that they can keep progressing through their routine without waiting for the shower (Deming, n.d.; Haines, 2000). I know that restructuring processes can be easily achieved through discussion, before making more costly data collection decisions. In practice I often encounter overlapping processes; that is reworks (Renger et al., 2018). I have to first ascertain whether the overlapping processes are necessary or whether they are in fact inefficiencies; that is, an unnecessary redundancy.

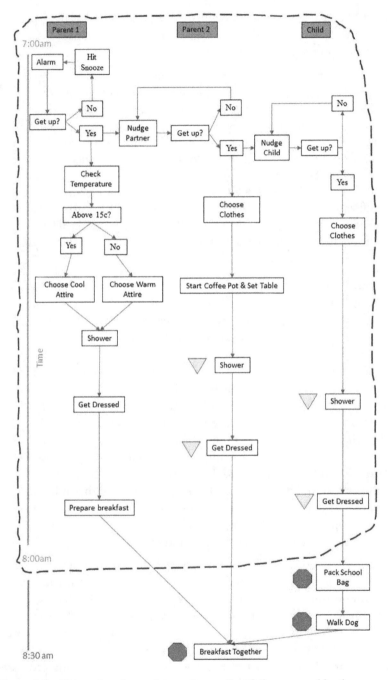

Figure 8.2 Illustrating the anticipated cascading failure caused by the over-lapping shower process.

To resolve this problem, I pull together the family members to discuss how their individual SOPs can be modified to accommodate each other (Renger et al., 2021). To help the family understand what the impact of changing their processes has on the other family members, I borrow my colleague Dr. Lewe Atkinson's Rubik's cube exercise. The Rubik's cube is a great visual to demonstrate interdependence: each move to align the color on one side (i.e., in an effort to get one's own processes in order) impacts all the other sides.

I then walk the family through their morning routine posing a series of "Now what?" and "What's next?" questions. This guided discussion helps each family member realize how her/his routine is impacting the processes of other family members. The exercise results in a modified JSOP. An example of how individual family processes were altered to remedy the cascading failure is shown in Figure 8.3. After the new JSOP is in place, I continue to look for other cascading failure trigger/choke points; places that if a process step fails, then everything downstream will collapse. I realize that the entire morning process depends on the alarm going off on time. Figure 8.4 depicts the scenario where the alarm clock fails to go off and the family wakes up 30-minutes late. Once again, the boxes with a yield sign symbol next to them denote a warning that processes are being delayed. The boxes with a stop sign symbol next to them signify that the processes will extend beyond the established time boundary. Essentially the entire routine is delayed by 30 minutes, making the goal of breakfast by 8:00 a.m. impossible.

> The dependence of an entire system on a single system trigger is not uncommon. The vulnerability of a system designed this way is obvious and often has disastrous effects. For example, in Hurricane Katrina the emergency response systems failed because higher level support systems did not receive a single phone call from the governor to set the support in motion (ABC News, 2005). In the Texas power outage, a similar problem was observed as the federal government response was delayed by 8 days waiting for an official emergency declaration form from the Texas governor (FEMA, n.d.). In both cases, the entire emergency response system failed to meet its emergent property of saving lives and property because of leadership's lack of understanding of their own processes.

I then fall back on my understanding of system attributes (Chapter 4) to offer the family two recommendations to prevent this cascading

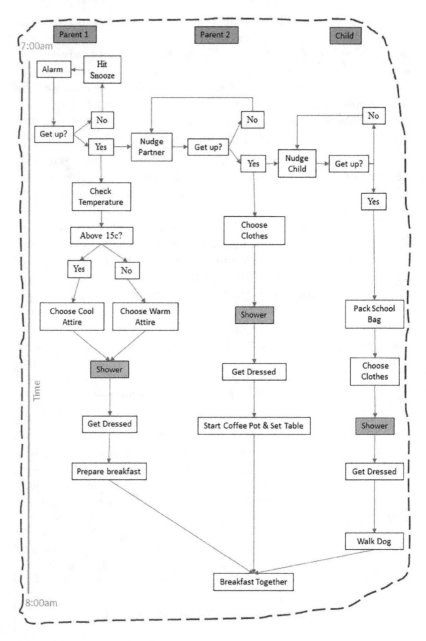

Figure 8.3 Modifying processes through discussion to improve system efficiency.

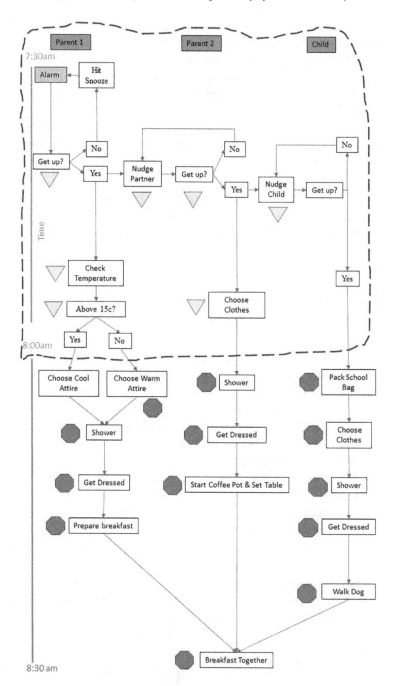

Figure 8.4 Anticipating a cascading system failure caused by an information system failure; the alarm clock.

failure (you will learn more about how to use system attributes to derive recommendations in Chapter 10). The first, training related, is to ensure Parent 1 knows how to set up and use the alarm. The second, technology related, is to set up a redundant system, for example by having each family member set their own alarm. In this system, a rework is a good thing! Since Parent 1 is confident he knows how to set up the alarm, the family opts to implement Option 2. The revised JSOPs, based on building in a redundant system to eliminate the cascading event, is shown in Figure 8.5.

> Bottlenecks, choke, or pinch points are obvious places to look for cascading events. Cascading events can occur within a system part SOP (Renger et al., 2017). However, in my experience they are most likely to occur between the seams, or in "handoffs" between system parts (Jackson et al., 2012; Renger et al., 2017). In reality, the failure to execute any system step has the potential to cause a cascading event, like failing to close a feedback loop. Just remember that should you detect a system breakdown; look upstream for the potential root cause (Vanden Heuvel, 2005).

Notice that my recommendations for preventing the two cascading failures are dependent on understanding the upstream cause. Although the cascading failure always causes a downstream ripple through the system, the recommendation is tied to the event trigger. In the case of the overlapping showers, my recommendation was to alter family processes. In the case where the alarm clock is the trigger event, my recommendation was to build in redundant information system infrastructure.

I then continue my careful review of the JSOPs, looking for feedback loops (Renger, 2016). Some feedback loops are not explicitly stated in the JSOP, but are implied. For example, I tacitly understand there is an information exchange happening between Parent 1 and the weather application used for checking the outside temperature (Figure 8.6). Without doing any additional data collection, I enquire whether the weather application is meeting the feedback criteria (e.g., closed, timely, credible, relevant, specific, sufficiently frequent).

After I've addressed as many efficiency problems as possible through a preliminary inspection, I allow time for the new processes

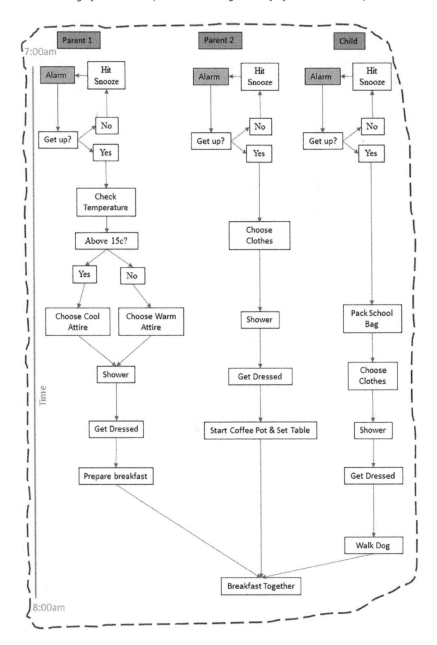

Figure 8.5 Revised JSOP based on solution for eliminating cascading failure trigger event (i.e., the alarm clock).

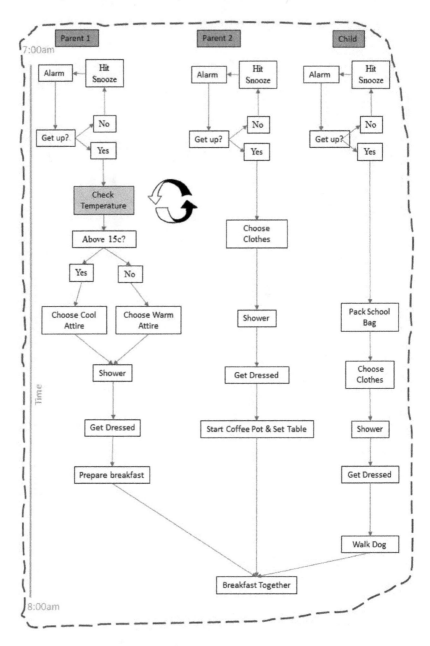

Figure 8.6 Identifying and evaluating a system feedback loop during the system scan.

to take hold and then meet with the family again to see whether the changes resulted in any improvements. Unfortunately, I learn the family continues to struggle to meet their goal of having breakfast together and they are still in disharmony. So, I decide it is necessary to invest in primary and secondary data collection to further evaluate where efficiencies can be realized. My preference is to try and observe the system in real time, either through direct observation or video, but that is obtrusive. Therefore, I supplement my evaluation with primary data, asking family members to keep written logs of their morning routine.

I then compare the family written logs to the JSOPs. By doing so I pinpoint two departures (denoted by an asterisk symbol in Figure 8.7) in the child's process steps that are causing delays. The first is that the child is playing video games. This was not in the original SOP and this added step is causing the child to be delayed in getting ready. The second, is that the child has repeated the process of dressing. This is a rework that is also adding time to the child's process.

I derive possible recommendations for the video game challenge by again drawing on my understanding of system attributes. The first, culture-based, is to have a family meeting to help reinforce the family's desire to achieve harmony through having breakfast together. The second recommendation, feedback loop driven, is to implement more frequent check-ins to make sure the child is progressing through the key steps of his/her routine in a timely manner.

To understand the reason why the child is redressing I follow-up with the child and engage in root cause analysis (Coşkun et al., 2012). I learn that the child is too young to understand how to translate the temperature information being relayed to her to choose the appropriate clothes. I think about suggesting adding a feedback loop to check whether the child is choosing the appropriate clothes, but I realize this can be time consuming and is dependent on the parent staying on top of the information exchange. I fall back on my understanding of a reflex arc to generate a better recommendation. I recommend empowering the child by giving her/him a tool to translate weather conditions into appropriate dress (see Figure 8.8). This bypass eliminates the need for the parents to micromanage their child's process and reinforces the "when in charge take charge" mantra (R. Hebb, personal communication, January 15, 2021). The new JSOP is shown in Figure 8.9.

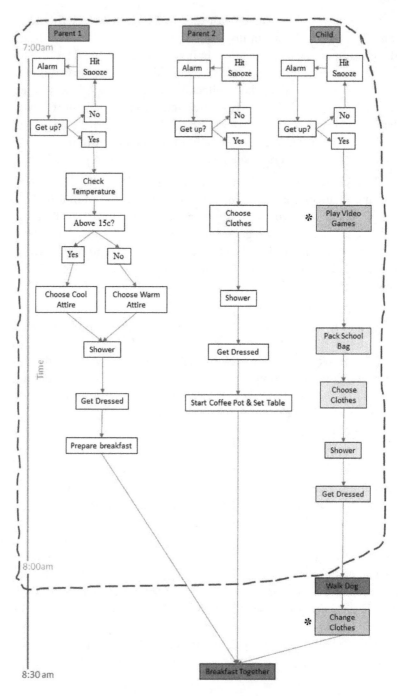

Figure 8.7 Delays in process steps detected through primary data collection.

Figure 8.8 A simple chart like this acts as a reflex arc, bypassing the need for constant parent input. https://ar.pinterest.com/pin/345299496420695057/

I then monitor the written logs to determine whether the new JSOPs are resulting in the intended efficiencies. I continue the evaluation process until there is evidence that the family consistently meets its interim goal of having breakfast together.

Once the family's morning routine is settled, I ask whether the family would like to expand the boundaries and begin evaluating their evening routine. The parents, pleased with the outcomes from the evaluation of the morning routine, indicate they would like to continue working on their evening routine. They establish the boundaries as the time they return from work and their child from school until they say their evening prayers. I repeat the process until similar efficiencies are obtained. There is no definitive length of time it can take for a system to adapt and routinely execute new SOPs. In practice I continue to monitor until the processes seem to be executed consistently for several weeks. Once the efficiencies are realized, I then turn my attention to evaluating whether family harmony (the emergent property) is achieved (see Chapter 9).

Conclusion

This chapter used a family systems example to reinforce how to apply system principles to define a system and evaluate system interdependencies. Regardless of the scale, level, or boundaries of the complex intervention acting as a system, the process for defining the system and evaluating efficiency is the same. That is, no matter how many family members are added, the process for defining and evaluating interdependencies remains the same. However, more family members do

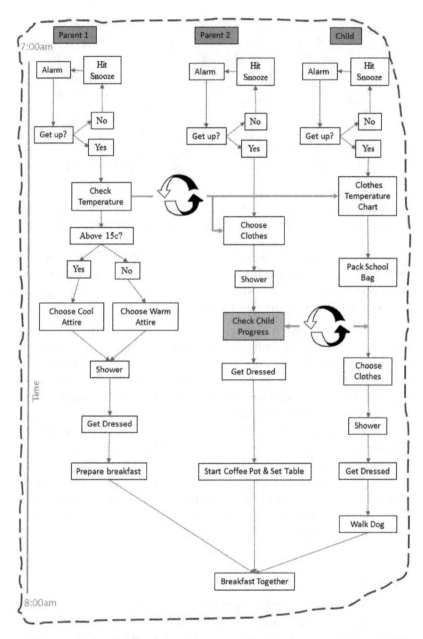

Figure 8.9 Using feedback loops and a reflex arc to address child SOP inefficiencies.

mean added complexity, so it will require more resources to define the SOPs and evaluate their interdependencies.

Systems principles such as cascading failures, feedback loops, and reflex arcs provide different perspectives for analyzing system part interdependencies. These principles can be evaluated during an initial scan of SOPs and by using primary or secondary data. The evaluation of system efficiencies (i.e., interdependencies) is an ongoing and iterative process; changes made to JSOPs need to be monitored to be sure they are having their desired effect. When this iterative process ends depends on the clients' resources and/or when system efficiency is optimized.

The efficient execution of interdependent system parts is a necessary prerequisite for the emergence of the essential system property and is the measure of system effectiveness. In the next chapter you will learn about how to evaluate system effectiveness, that is the system's emergent property.

References

ABC News. (2005, September 6). *Who's to blame for delayed response to Katrina?* https://abcnews.go.com/WNT/HurricaneKatrina/blame-delayed -response-katrina/story?id=1102467

Coşkun, R., Akande, A., & Renger, R. (2012). Using root cause analysis for evaluating program improvement. *Evaluation Journal of Australasia, 12*(2), 4–14. https://doi.org/10.1177/1035719X1201200202

Deming, W. E. (n.d.). *Quote: Every system is perfectly designed to get the results it gets.* https://deming.org/quotes/10141/

FEMA. (n.d.). *Declared disasters.* https://www.fema.gov/disaster/declarations

Haines, S. G. (2000). *The systems thinking approach to strategic planning and management.* St. Lucie Press.

Jackson, B. A., Faith, K. S., & Willis, H. H. (2012). Evaluating the reliability of emergency response systems for large-scale incident operations. *Rand Health Quarterly, 2*(3), 8. https://www.rand.org/pubs/periodicals/ health-quarterly/issues/v2/n3/08.html

Make Mealtime Family Time. (n.d.). www.makemealtimefamilytime.com

Meadows, D. (2008). *Thinking in systems: A primer.* Chelsea Green Publishing.

Renger, R. (2016). Illustrating the evaluation of system feedback mechanisms using system evaluation theory (SET). *Evaluation Journal of Australasia, 16*(4), 15–21. https://doi.org/10.1177/1035719X1601600403

Renger, R., Foltysova, J., Ienuso, S., Renger, J., & Booze, W. (2017). Evaluating system cascading failures. *Evaluation Journal of Australasia, 17*(2), 29–36. https://doi.org/10.1177/1035719X1701700205

Renger, R., Keogh, B., Hawkins, A., Foltysova, K., & Souvannasacd, E. (2018). Reworks: A robust system efficiency measure. *Evaluation Journal of Australasia, 18*(3), 183–191. https://doi.org/10.1177/1035 719X18796611

Renger, R., McPherson, M., Kontz-Bartels, T., & Becker, K. (2016). Process flow mapping for systems improvement: Lessons learned. *The Canadian Journal of Program Evaluation,* 31, 109–121.

Renger, R., Renger, J., Basson, M. D., Van Eck, R., Renger, J., Souvannasacd, E., & Hart, G. (2021). Using the Homeland Security and Exercise Evaluation Program (HSEEP) building block approach to implement system evaluation theory (SET). *American Journal of Evaluation, 42*(4), 586–601. https://doi.org/10.1177/1098214020986619

Vanden Heuvel, L. N. (2005). *Root cause analysis handbook: A guide to effective incident investigation.* ABS Consulting.

Yarbrough, D. B. (2017). Developing the program utility standards: Scholarly foundations and collaborative processes. *Canadian Journal of Program Evaluation, 31*(3), 284–304. https://doi.org/10.3138/cjpe.349

9

Systems Evaluation Theory Step 3, Evaluating System Effectiveness (Emergence)

Life's not linear nor reducible to disconnected parts,
and your evaluation shouldn't be either!

—Pescud (personal communication, September 21, 2021)

Having some assurance that the complex intervention acting as a system is operating efficiently, you can now invest in evaluating its effectiveness. To evaluate a system's emergent property is to evaluate its effectiveness. Throughout this book I provided examples of emergent system properties. However, the failure to understand a system's emergent property has significant consequences on evaluation, usually adding unnecessary cost by engaging in nonsensical, reductionist-driven, analyses. Therefore, to help solidify what is meant by a system's emergent property I begin this chapter by providing a few more additional, practical

System Evaluation Theory, pages 159–173
Copyright © 2022 by Information Age Publishing
www.infoagepub.com
All rights of reproduction in any form reserved.

examples, that last of which may surprise you! I then reflect on challenges I have faced in trying to evaluate the emergent property of systems.

Additional Examples of System Emergent Properties

Fiction Writing

A successful fiction novel engrosses the reader and transports her/him to another place. Oatley (2011), a fiction novelist and psychologist, refers to this emergent property as a dream state. No system part, no single letter of a word, no single word of a sentence, no sentence of a paragraph, no paragraph of a chapter, and no chapter by itself can achieve the emergent system property. The writer's challenge is to have all these system elements, working together at different levels, come together so that Oatley's dream state will emerge.

If one were to evaluate a fiction novel, then it would be meaningless to ask readers about individual system parts, like letters, words, paragraphs, or a chapter. Rather, to evaluate the emergence of the dream state you might ask readers about whether they got "lost" in the story, or whether they "lost track of time" while reading the book.

A concept related to the emergent system property is the Tibetan Buddhist concept of the emptiness of inherent existence. Take a book for example. There's nothing in a book that tells you it is a book. The book does not assert its own reality. A book is the trees from which it came, a technical by-product, the history of the printing press, and a tool for the recording of thoughts and stories, amongst many other things. We have given it a word and function within the dependent open system in which we're embedded. A book exists within a vast continuum of interdependent parts. It does not exist without these, thus it is empty of inherent existence (Pescud, personal email communication, February 15, 2022).

Sports Teams

Like many of you reading this book, I was not trained as an evaluator. I completed my doctorate in sports psychology. Not being able to find stable employment I fell into evaluation; a fall I do not regret.

In sports, coaches hope to assemble the correct mix of team parts to achieve "chemistry," or as it is better known in sports psychology, team cohesion (Di Onofrio et al., 2019). Team cohesion depends on the interdependent interactions between coaches–players, players–players, players–nutrition, and factors outside the system (e.g., owners, fans, and the media). Like Ackoff's (1994) car example, just having the best parts, that is, the most skilled players, does not translate into team cohesion. Evaluating team cohesion at an individual level is meaningless; rather team cohesion must be evaluated at a higher, team level, for example, by examining the presence of "network relationships" (Brave et al., 2018).

With respect to sports teams, there may also be a second emergent property. Recall in Chapter 4, I made the case that perhaps culture is also a ubiquitous emergent system property. Many coaches argue that it is in fact the team culture that they are striving to build. For example, Tony Dungy (2022), a well-known NFL coach noted, "A coach's job is not just X's and O's, a coach's job is to build the culture, that's the key to winning" (January 15).

The Tax System

Can there be anything more complex than a tax system? Over the years several staff members from the Australian Tax Office have attended my systems evaluation workshops. Initially we struggled to define the emergent property of the tax system. However, over many a coffee and breakfast we eventually reasoned that the emergent property is *fairness*. When all the tax laws, codes, and officials are working together as they should then a tax burden that is fair for all members of society should emerge.

Surprise!! Evaluation

Mel Mark, Gary Henry, and the late George Julnes argued that the ultimate goal of evaluation is social betterment (Henry, 2003; Henry & Mark, 2003; Mark et al., 2000; Mark & Henry, 2004). These authors emphasize the need for evaluations to consider different analysis levels (individual, interpersonal, and collective) and processes (general influence, attitudinal, motivational, behavioral) if it [the evaluation] is to achieve the ultimate goal of social betterment. Even though the authors never use the terms system or systems thinking, I would argue that this sounds very much like interdependence and emergence!

The authors also formulated an *integrated* theory of evaluation ([ITOE]; Mark et al., 2000). The ITOE discusses the need for evaluators to consider four evaluation purposes: oversight and compliance; program improvement; merit and worth; and knowledge development. I think it would be fair to say that the ITOE rests on the premise that the *interdependence* between different evaluation purposes is necessary for social betterment to *emerge*. For example, if an intervention is shown to have little impact, then it is important to know whether the intervention was delivered with fidelity to decide on an appropriate recommendation (Renger et al., 2013). When these evaluation purposes are working together in harmony there is a greater likelihood that recommendations leading to social betterment will emerge. So, you see, evaluation when done correctly is also steeped in systems thinking, it's just that evaluators don't typically think in these terms!

As an aside, Dr. Mel Mark, who I cited above, was influential in my early days as an evaluator, mentoring me as I worked through my first peer reviewed publication in the *American Journal of Evaluation*. We all need someone who will take us under their wing at different points in our career. I will forever be indebted to him for guiding me through the publication process.

Considerations in Evaluating Emergence

When I embarked on my systems journey the first challenge was to help my clients understand and define the emergent system property. Getting leaders to think beyond outputs is critical and often a challenge (Reed, 2006). Using some of the aforementioned examples in this chapter as well as those provided in Chapters 2 and 6 have proven useful in helping my clients understand and define their own system's emergent property. Once the emergent system property is defined, you can then shift to determining the best way it can be evaluated. I now share three considerations in evaluating a system's emergent property, the need to: (a) avoid reductionist thinking, (b) consider the multidimensionality of the emergent essential system property, and (c) ascertain who has responsibility for evaluating the system's essential emergent property.

Avoid Reductionist Thinking, Instead Think Synthesis

By far, the most frequent and passionate debates I encounter when discussing evaluating system emergence are from quantitative researchers/evaluators trained in a reductionist worldview (Renger, 2014). Reductionists want to evaluate system success by dissecting the system into parts (Brant, 2010). They argue that people want to know what parts of the system are working. They point to statistics like multiple regression that can be used to establish the unique proportion of variation each part accounts in the system (Volk et al., 2016). However, their reasoning is fundamentally flawed because the assumptions underlying the statistics are not consistent with the basic premise of a system. In fact, one the underlying assumptions of multiple regression is independence between variables, quite the opposite of interdependence, to which Melanie

Pescud (personal communication, November 2, 2021) quipped, "[Statistics like multiple regression] deny the existence of interdependence and emergence." As you know from Chapter 2, system parts must work together interdependently for the system property to emerge, therefore it is *meaningless* to treat parts of a complex intervention acting as a system as independent contributors to an outcome.

Another problem is the tendency of reductionists to equate the success of a system part with the success of the system as a whole. Take homelessness as an example. Homelessness is a symptom of a larger problem and has many determinants (Busch-Geertsema, 2013). A person's homelife, education, job skills, environment, and so on all interact to create destabilization. It is the lack of *stability* that is at the heart of what we have labeled homelessness (O. Passons, personal communication, October 28, 2021). To understand this requires synthesis thinking, seeing the whole picture. Nevertheless, some researchers judge the success of complex homelessness interventions by whether a person was provided a house, or as it is referred to by those working in the sector "heads in beds" (Veness, 1992). While providing a house is important, it is but one small part of the system needed for stabilization to emerge. Defining system success as whether a person has a house oversimplifies, and completely misses, the reality of the situation (Volk et al., 2016). To solve homelessness requires the coordination and co-operation of many parts of the social system that normally work in silos (Greenberg & Rosenheck, 2010).

I gave a talk entitled "The Wolf (researcher) in Sheep's (evaluator's) Clothing" at the Canadian Evaluation Society conference in 2014 (Renger, 2014). I encountered a rather hostile audience. Many in the room argued that "randomized control trials are the only way to know whether a program works." I could have packed it in that day but I didn't. I share this story to remind you to stay strong and steady in your resolve to promote and use systems approaches even when you encounter opposition!

Evaluate the Multidimensionality of the Emergent Essential System Property

A system's essential property is often multidimensional, a reflection of the complexity of the system from which it emerges. Customer experience, team cohesion, the dream state, quality of life, fairness, and so forth are multidimensional. This multidimensionality is often mirrored in the evaluation tools, such as a lengthy survey instrument consisting of numerous questions and subscales. The problem is such tools, usually developed for research purposes, are often impractical for evaluation purposes. Most of my clients do not have the time or resources to invest in primary data collection using lengthy survey instruments.

One alternative to survey data collection is to use proxies, or indicators, of the emergent system property. Indicators vary on a continuum from subjective (e.g., it feels hot outside) to objective (e.g., it is 45°C; Rogerson et al., 1989). They can be collected using a variety of methods. For example, Orpana et al. (2016) identified 39 indicators for age-friendly communities. Many of the indicators can be gathered through direct observation (e.g., number of accessible washrooms) or are available in secondary data sets (e.g., crime fraud data). As another example, Andreassen (1994) defined willingness to return to the business as an indicator of customer satisfaction and loyalty. For example, customer receipts, a secondary dataset, could be used as a proxy of customer loyalty.

Of course, indicators will not always be available and/or you may need to incorporate multiple indicators to capture the essence of the emergent system property. In some cases, you may simply not know how to measure a system's emergent property! For example, while social betterment is an emergent evaluation system property, I could find no indicators nor data on its measurement. One suggestion I have is to partner with psychologists and sociologists who are experts at developing tools for evaluating multidimensional constructs. I have always taught that knowing what to measure is the essential first step, but you may not always know how to measure it. No one said it would be easy!

One regret in my career is that I did not take more sociology and anthropology courses. Both these disciplines place a greater emphasis on systems and engage in synthesis to understand collective behavior and social problems: a much better fit for systems thinking. My training in psychology was steeped in understanding individual behavior using a reductionist paradigm.

Ascertain Who Has Responsibility for Evaluating the System's Essential Emergent Property

I have evaluated numerous local, county, state, and federal initiatives during my career. A common theme is that the responsibility for data collection always seems to get passed down to the lowest system level. The problem is the lowest system level may not be the correct level to be collecting data on the emergent system property. In all honesty I believe this strategy is often about avoiding responsibility rather than determining who is best situated to collect needed data.

For example, for several years I oversaw the evaluation of the Arizona Area Health Education Center (AHEC). AHEC's focus is on addressing the shortage of healthcare professionals in medically underserved areas (e.g., rural and inner-city). AHECs are funded by the Bureau of Health Professions (BHPr), which resides in the Health Resources and Services Administration; a federal department. BHPr passes the responsibility for collecting data on health care shortages down to the state programs. Each AHEC state program consists of several regional offices. Each AHEC state program then passes the responsibility of collecting data on health care shortages to the regional offices.

Despite numerous decades of funding, evaluations of AHECs have shown minimal impact, and the health care shortage has persisted and continues to grow (West et al., 2007). "Why?" Common sense suggests there are many influences that act upon a person's decision to choose a health care profession and to then work in a medically underserved area. For example, the quality of schools, spousal employment opportunities, and autonomy in a small community, are just some of the factors that significantly influence whether a health care professional settles in a medically underserved area. The problem is that many of these are beyond the control of an AHEC to change (Renger, 2006).

A concerted effort, requiring the coordination of multiple programs, each targeting important aspects of the healthcare professional shortage is needed to match the complexity of the problem. Thus, not only do all the AHEC regional and state programs need to be coordinated, but so too do all the programs housed under the BHPr umbrella. While each program should be held accountable for evaluating its immediate contributions to the emergent property, the responsibility for evaluating the emergent system property must reside at the population level (Friedman, 2005) and should be the responsibility of the Department of Health and Human Services to evaluate.

One positive example of understanding the appropriate level of system data collection occurs within the Centers for Disease Control and Prevention (CDC). One cancer screening program I evaluated asks local and state partners to collect data on the success of screening rates. Increasing preventive screening is one important part of reducing the cancer burden. However, there are many other programs housed under the CDC targeting other aspects of cancer burden. Therefore, it is the CDC, a national entity, that assumes responsibility for tracking cancer rates nationwide over time. This data collection burden is not passed down to system parts (i.e., individual programs).

Emergence Strength

When I first heard the terms strong emergence and weak emergence, I assumed it meant that an emergent system property could be placed on a continuum. The better the system parts work together interdependently, I thought, the stronger the system emergent property. For example, the better each word, sentence, paragraph, and chapter work together the more likely the reader will be lost in a dream state.

However, according to Chalmers (2006), the difference between strong and weak emergence has to do with expectations. Weak emergence occurs when you can perhaps reason what might be expected when interdependent system parts interact. Strong emergence, according to Chalmers, is when you can't predict the emergent property from the parts.

> In full transparency I believe the emergent properties I have defined with clients in doing system evaluation work is mostly weak, by Chalmers' (2006) definition. That is, my clients, with my guidance, can reason and somewhat predict what the system parts are trying to achieve together. I believe this to be a very reasonable starting point in trying to evaluate system effectiveness, but I do think we must continually be vigilant so that we might uncover an unanticipated, or strongly emergent property.

To illustrate the difference between weak and strong emergence, imagine how a transportation system might begin to evolve. Working with leadership you might initially define the emergent system property as something like public confidence in moving from point A to B. This emergent property may be relatively easy to predict, so by Chalmer's (2006) definition it is a weakly emergent property.

To evaluate public confidence, one could use a traditional survey, but this is a costly endeavor. Using an indicator like the number of monthly passes sold, might be an inexpensive alternative of public confidence in the transportation system because it is an available secondary data set. However, for argument's sake assume that we don't observe any change in the sale of monthly passes. We might, therefore, conclude that the system is ineffective in creating public confidence. However, because of our understanding of strong emergence we should consider whether we are tapping into the correct system emergent property. For example, it might be that the emergent system property isn't rider confidence, rather it might be something like the rider experience. Poorly maintained, dirty buses, trains, and subways, can create a negative rider experience and deter riders from using the transportation system.

Another example of weak and strong emergence comes from my experience as a sports psychologist. Earlier in this chapter I used team cohesion as an example of an emergent property. Team cohesion is common knowledge in sports circles and thus I could probably predict with some certainty that team leaders would identify this as the emergent property. This would be a weakly emergent system property.

On the other hand, a somewhat unpredictable outcome, a strongly emergent property, might be the genuine love players express and feel for their teammates. As Vince Lomardi said, "Teamwork is what the Green Bay Packers are all about. They didn't do it for individual glory. They did it because they loved one another" (LaForce, n.d., opening quote). Interestingly, LaForce (n.d.) cites several indicators of how love for one's teammates might be evaluated including "fiercely defending each other against all threats, arguing but knowing the relationship was fine, showing a teammate that failed they were still a valued member of the team, shared the pain of their teammates, and so forth" (para. 3).

> These examples highlight an important learning point about evaluating emergence. Even though starting with leadership to define a systems emergent property makes sense for a number of reasons (e.g., cost, buy-in), the failure to see evidence of the emergent property may signal they need to engage a broader range of system actors, including those who are the target of the complex intervention, to gain their perspectives to perhaps discover a stronger, unexpected emergent property.

More Than One Emergent System Property?

During one of my 2021 AES workshops a participant asked a very insightful question: "Can a system have more than one emergent property?" I don't have any sound theoretical evidence, but empirically speaking I suspect that systems can have more than one emergent property. In the transportation example above feelings of safety may be another strongly emergent property. Keeping your mind open to the possibility of there being more than one emergent property is important, but in evaluation practice it is hard enough to define and agree on a single emergent system property, never mind multiple emergent properties. However, if you have identified more than one emergent property it is unlikely you will have the resources to evaluate them all, so you will need to engage leadership to help you prioritize which to evaluate.

A Reflective Learning Example

HUD HOPE VI—What Could I Have Done Differently Had I Known Then What I Know Now?

One of my first evaluation projects in the late 1990s was to evaluate the U.S. Department of Housing and Urban Development (HUD) Housing Opportunity for People Everywhere (HOPE) initiative in Tucson, Arizona (HUD, n.d.). The main goal of the HOPE program was to undo the disaster that was the public housing experiment that emerged as a result of the National Housing Act of 1934. The HOPE program consisted of many components, such as reducing housing density by relocating willing residents, tax incentives to avoid being displaced due to gentrification, improving neighborhood safety by adding green spaces and lighting, expanding education and life skills programs for residents, and so forth.

As a neophyte I developed logic models for each of the components; after all I was trained as a reductionist researcher. I then developed and published methods, like using geographic information systems, to evaluate these component goals (Renger et al., 2002). At the time I recall being quite proud of my evaluation. The evaluation did help to secure two additional HOPE grants, which was unheard of for a community the size of Tucson. In some ways these additional grants could have been considered an evaluation success, because they led to social betterment! More families were living in better conditions, right?

In hindsight, I really feel I missed the boat with respect to evaluating the HOPE project. The HOPE project was conceptually well thought out, understanding that giving people a new house wasn't enough, they needed education, job opportunities, and support to avoid their new community being taken over by outsiders. The HOPE framework outlined the need for the integration of all these components. My evaluation strategy, unfortunately, did not match this conceptualization. In fact, I had imposed my limited way of looking at the world to the problem at hand; I was engaging in single-loop thinking (Chapter 4) forcing the proverbial square peg into a round hole.

As I look back now, through my systems thinking lens, it is clear to me that I should have viewed the HOPE component parts as interdependent and thus asked the question, "What is expected to emerge?" I think this line of inquiry with leadership might have led to an understanding of quality of life or stability as emergent system properties. Since each HOPE grant targeted about 200 families, it certainly would have been feasible to evaluate these emergent system properties in all project participants.

I imagine now how different the results might have looked and the different conclusions I might have reached. By focusing my evaluation on the interdependence between system parts I could have answered more meaningful questions like, "Do the job skills being taught match the neighborhood employment opportunities?" and/or "Were the public spaces encouraging resident interaction and feelings of safety?" By focusing on emergence, I could have answered a question like, "Were people who chose to relocate experiencing a better quality of life than those who chose to stay in their neighborhood?" These questions would have been far more meaningful than reporting on a reduction in housing density, the number of new jobs created, the number of people completing GED, and so on. I also shudder at the lost opportunity the influence of my evaluation could have had nationwide if other HOPE evaluations adopted a systems perspective too. It is my intention that by sharing this reflective example that you too will take the time to look back upon pieces of evaluation work you have completed considering where a system thinking lens would have been more appropriate and ultimately helpful to the communities it sought to serve.

Be careful not to judge a book by its cover! The HOPE "program" wasn't a program at all, it was a complex intervention acting as a system! On the other hand, what some may be labeling as a "system" may just be a "bunch of stuff." Always do the systems test.

Conclusion

Within systems evaluation theory, the process of defining and evaluating a complex intervention acting as a system begins (Chapter 6) and ends with emergence (Chapter 9). Beginning with an understanding of emergence is like setting the system's North Star. Once that is set, it makes sense to understand the needed system parts, how they need to work interdependently, and eventually whether they are successful in achieving what they set out to do.

As noted earlier in this book, you should not be surprised at how much disagreement exists among system actors at all levels as to what they believe they are trying to accomplish together that they cannot do individually. I believe it is our job as evaluators to facilitate system actors putting the dots together to see the bigger, emerging picture.

Emergent properties are often multidimensional and, as a consequence, may be difficult to evaluate. However, just because it may be difficult to evaluate does not justify reducing the evaluation of the system effectiveness to an evaluation of its parts. Such an evaluation of system effectiveness is nonsensical from a systems perspective. An effort must be made to evaluate the emergent property. The tools and indicators to do so may not be readily available, but that should not deter us from trying or being creative in our efforts. Further, the responsibility for evaluating the emergent property cannot fall on individual system parts, it must be the responsibility of those overseeing the system, which is often the next highest system level, be it the population or community level.

References

Andreassen, T. W. (1994). Satisfaction, loyalty, and reputation as indicators of customer orientation in the public sector. *International al Journal of Public Sector Management, 7*(2), 16–34. https://doi.org/10.1108/09513559410055206

Brant, S. (2010, October 23). *If Russ Ackoff had given a TED talk* [Video]. YouTube. https://www.youtube.com/watch?v=OqEeIG8aPPk

Brave, S. A., Butters, R. A., & Roberts, K. A. (2018). *In search of the holy grail: Team chemistry and where to find it.*

Busch-Geertsema, V. (2013). *Housing first Europe final report.* European Union Programme for Employment and Social Security. https://www.habitat.hu/files/FinalReportHousingFirstEurope.pdf

Chalmers, D. J. (2006). *Strong and weak emergence.* Australian National University. www.consc.net/papers/emergence.pdf

Di Onofrio, V., Montesano, P., & Mazzeo, F. (2019). Physical-technical conditions, coaching and nutrition: An integrated approach to promote cohesion in sports teams. *Journal of Human Sport and Exercise, 14*(Proc4), S981–S990. https://doi.org/10.14198/jhse.2019.14.Proc4.60

Dungy, T. (2022, January 15). *NFL Football Preshow* [TV Series]. NBC.

Friedman, M. (2005). *Trying hard is not good enough: How to produce measurable improvements for customers and communities.* Trafford.

Greenberg, G. A., & Rosenheck, R. A. (2010). An evaluation of an initiative to improve coordination and service delivery of homeless services networks. *The Journal of Behavioral Health Services & Research, 37,* 184–196. https://doi.org/10.1007/s11414-008-9164-9

Henry, G. T. (2003). Influential Evaluations. *American Journal of Evaluation, 24*(4), 515–524. https://doi.org/10.1177/109821400302400409

Henry, G. T., & Mark, M. (2003). Beyond use: Understanding evaluation's influence on attitudes and actions. *American Journal of Evaluation, 24*(3), 293–314. https://doi.org/10.1177/109821400302400302

LaForce, T. (n.d.). *Love your teammates.* https://tomlaforce.com/love-your -teammates/

Mark, M. M., & Henry G. T. (2004). The mechanisms and outcomes of evaluation influence. *Evaluation, 10*(1), 35–57. https://doi.org/10 .1177/1356389004042326

Mark, M. M., Henry, G. T., & Julnes, G. (2000). *Evaluation: An integrated framework for understanding, guiding, and improving policies and programs.* Jossey-Bass.

Oatley, K (2011). *Such stuff as dreams: The psychology of fiction.* John Wiley and Sons. https://doi.org/10.1002/9781119970910

Orpana, H., Chawla, M., Gallagher, E., & Escaravage E. (2016). Developing indicators for evaluation of age-friendly communities in Canada: Process and results. *Health Promotion and Chronic Disease Prevention Canada, 36*(10), 214–223. https://doi.org/10.24095/hpcdp.36.10.02

Reed, G. E. (2006). Leadership and systems thinking. *Defense AT&L, 35*(3), 10–13.

Renger R. (2006). Consequences to federal programs when the logic-modeling process is not followed with fidelity. *American Journal of Evaluation, 27*(4), 452–463. https://doi.org/10.1177/1098214006293666

Renger, R. (2014). *The wolf (researcher) in sheep's (evaluator's) clothing.* Canadian Evaluation Society Annual Conference, Ottawa, Canada.

Renger, R., Cimetta, A., Pettygrove, S., & Rogan, S. (2002). Geographic information systems (GIS) as an evaluation tool. *American Journal of Evaluation, 23*(4), 469–479. https://doi.org/10.1177/109821400202300407

Renger, R., Bartel, G., & Foltysova, J. (2013). The reciprocal relationship between implementation theory and program theory in assisting decision-making. *Canadian Journal of Program Evaluation, 28*(1), 27–41.

Rogerson, R. J., Findlay, A. M., Morris, A. S., & Coombes, M. G. (1989). Indicators of quality of life: Some methodological issues. *Environment and Planning A: Economy and Space, 21*(12), 1655–1666. https://doi .org/10.1068/a211655

U.S. Department of Housing and Urban Development. (n.d.). *HOPE VI.* https://www.hud.gov/program_offices/public_indian_housing/ programs/ph/hope6

Veness, A. R. (1992). Home and homelessness in the United States: Changing ideals and realities. *Environment and Planning D: Society and Space, 10*(4), 445–468. https://doi.org/10.1068/d100445

Volk, J. S., Aubry, T., Goering, P., Adair, C. E., Distasio, J., Jette, J., Nolin, D., Stergiopoulos, V., Streiner, D. L., & Tsemberis, S. (2016). Tenants with additional needs: When housing first does not solve

homelessness. *Journal of Mental Health, 25*(2), 169–175, https://doi
.org/10.3109/09638237.2015.1101416

West, E. A., Griffith, W. P., & Iphofen, R. (2007). A historical perspective on
the nursing shortage. *Medsurg Nursing, 16*(2), 124–130.

10

Deriving Recommendations

Actions speak louder than words.

As you learned in the previous chapter, some evaluators believe the success of an evaluation should be judged by its ability to meet a higher purpose of social betterment; an emergent evaluation property (Henry, 2000, 2003; Henry & Mark, 2003; Mark et al., 2000). However, other evaluators argue that evaluation use, or utility, should be the gold standard of evaluation success (Patton, 2008; Yarbrough, 2017).

> Evaluation use is defined as "the intentional and serious consideration of evaluation information by an individual with the potential to act on it" (King & Pechman, 1982, p. 40).

It is my position that these two perspectives are not different "camps" per se, but rather evaluation use is a necessary prerequisite for social betterment. If evaluation findings are not used, then social betterment is not possible.

System Evaluation Theory, pages 175–188
Copyright © 2022 by Information Age Publishing
www.infoagepub.com
175

There are many factors influencing whether evaluation findings are seriously considered (McCormick, 1997; Patton, 2008). Some of these factors, like the politics of a commission, are not within the control of the evaluator. However, one factor that is within the evaluator's control is the *type* of evaluation information being provided to those with the potential to act.

Some evaluators believe that the type of information provided to decision-makers should be restricted to the evaluation findings. The argument from these evaluators is that "their responsibilities [should be] limited to designing the study, collecting the data, and providing the results in a final report; the use of those results is entirely the responsibility of the decision-maker. Technical quality and methodological rigor, rather than the use of the results, [should be] the primary criteria by which evaluation studies [are] judged" (McCormick, 1997, p. 1).

The position that the evaluator's responsibility ends at providing the evaluation findings is rooted in the value-free doctrine (Scriven, 1991). To be value-free means the evaluator must be objective and not let her/his values influence the evaluation (Scriven, 1991). While this doctrine was shown to be utter nonsense decades ago (Gray, 1968), it continued into the 1990s (Scriven, 1991), and in my experience, based on listening to evaluation presentations worldwide, it is still a pervasive view among many evaluators. It is simply impossible for any line of inquiry not to be influenced by the scientist [evaluator] doing the inquiry. As Scriven (1991) wrote, "The scientist's personal values play an important role in affecting their choice of field and of explanatory models and that science has social consequences" (p. 2).

I am among those evaluators who believe that one way we bring value to evaluation is by extending the type of evaluation information presented to decision-makers from simple findings to actionable recommendations.

> A recommendation is defined as "a suggestion as to the best course of action, especially one put forward by an authoritative body" (https://www.lexico.com/en/definition/recommendation).

Our clients look to us [evaluators] as the authoritative body; they look to us to bring meaning to evaluation findings through our appreciation of context synthesized into a recommendation. A recommendation conveys to decision-makers the seriousness of the evaluation. By definition, a recommendation forces the consideration of evaluation information because it implores the decision-makers to make a decision about a course of action.

> To limit evaluation reports to the findings is, in my opinion, a dereliction of duty. Afterall, the root of the word evaluation is value! To synthesize data with context to arrive at a recommendation requires systems thinking and is value-added for the client. I postulated many reasons why some evaluators choose to stop short of providing recommendations including that they are using the value-free doctrine as a shield against being held accountable (Renger et al., 2022).

Presenting evaluation findings and making recommendations are not mutually exclusive. Evaluations should be done with the greatest degree of quality to generate the most accurate findings (Yarbrough et al., 2010). These data together with an appreciation of context need to then be synthesized into a recommendation. The decision-maker may not agree with the recommendation, but at least by providing a recommendation it encourages the decision-maker to think about the evaluation and what it means.

Making recommendations requires evaluator self-efficacy. If you follow systems evaluation theory (SET), then you can have the confidence that the evaluation approach, the findings, and the recommendations will be worth considering. I now share with you some considerations in deriving recommendations for improving the efficiency and effectiveness of complex interventions operating and functioning as systems, respectively.

Deriving Recommendations for Improving System Efficiency

As you now know from Chapters 7 and 8, system inefficiencies are detected by comparing observed system processes against the system standard of acceptability, joint system operating procedures. A detected inefficiency *is* an evaluation finding. The next step, then, is to offer a recommendation about how to address the system inefficiency.

I view a recommendation as a form of client feedback. Thus, when formulating and providing recommendations I am sensitive to the criteria used to judge feedback quality you learned about in Chapter 7; ensuring the recommendations are relevant, specific, timely, sufficiently frequent, and credible.

Recommendation Relevance

Relevant is defined as "closely connected or appropriate to what is being done and considered" (https://www.lexico.com/definition/relevant). Since SET is an evaluation approach that is purposely designed to define and evaluate complex interventions acting as systems, there is an excellent likelihood that recommendations forthcoming from the approach will align with the decision-makers' understanding of the reality in which the intervention operates and functions. For example, system efficiency recommendations, like closing a communication loop, eliminating a redundancy, and introducing a bypass are rooted in an understanding of system part interdependencies. Thus, such recommendations are more likely to align with system decision-makers' day-to-day experience. If results make sense, that is, they resonate with the decision-makers' understanding of the situation, then they are more likely to be used (Barlow & Stone, 2011; Byrne, 2019).

Recommendation Specificity

Recommendations need to meet two conditions related to specificity; pinpointing both the cause and solution of the system inefficiency. In Chapter 7 you learned about how to use system principles to pinpoint the cause(s) of inefficient system interdependencies. Thus, the first condition for specificity is met.

To meet the second specificity condition, I recommend searching for a solution to an observed system inefficiency by first looking to the four system attributes you learned about in Chapter 4 (i.e., leadership, culture, information systems, and training). The rationale for starting with the four attributes is simple; if the four attributes are necessary for system efficiency at all levels, then by definition their absence might be the reason for a system inefficiency. For example, one finding in my evaluation of a Center for Translational Research was that the system parts had trouble coordinating. In applying the four attributes, it became immediately obvious that the problem was culturally based; the system parts had never been asked to work together before. The recommendation to leadership was to begin reinforcing a system culture and to support an evaluation strategy aimed at simultaneously building a culture of coordination (Renger et al., 2021).

I could have started my search for recommendations by looking for ways to improve system processes and structures. However, as per the Haines' systems pyramid (Chapter 4) all things systems rest on culture, so it is a logical place to begin when deriving a recommendation.

If none of the four system attributes seem to be the root cause of the inefficiency, then I recommend methodically applying the system principles you learned in Chapter 7 (i.e., feedback loops, cascading failures, reflex arcs, and reworks) to see whether they might offer a suggested path forward to make improvements in the system structures and processes. In terms of Haines' iceberg model, I work my way up the pyramid from bottom to top. For example, in evaluating the points of dispensing exercise (Chapter 7), I first looked at whether lack of training was the cause for the back up at one of the processing stations. After concluding that it wasn't a training issue, I then used my understanding of cascading failures to pinpoint the source of the problem. My recommendation was simply to address the identified source of the problem, in this case more specific feedback to the public messaging regarding points of dispensing appointment times.

Another way to increase recommendation specificity is to suggest simple, order generating rules as corrective actions. Recall from Chapter 3 that simple, order generating rules can often underpin what seems to be complex system behavior (Burnes, 2005; Friederici, 2009) and "heightens the likelihood that systems level outcomes will emerge (Foster-Fishman & Watson, 2011, p. 514). Examples of simple, order generating rules I've recommended include asking the incident commander to close all 213 requests within 24 hours (Chapter 7), requiring all health screening contractors to always go to the state website to be sure they are using the most current data collection form (Chapter 3), and asking decision-makers to respond to my recommendations within 1 week.

Some evaluators have pushed back on my use of near real-time (NRT) evaluation. When I ask why they are reluctant, they say they need to collect sufficient observations to be certain that change in outcomes can be attributed to intervention. This type of reductionist thinking is killing our field. Such certainty is needed in the research phase of knowledge development. However, when we evaluate the application of that knowledge via interventions we need to stop thinking like researchers and start thinking like evaluators. Sometimes, we just need to use common sense. Michael Scriven classically threw a bottle across a room once and remarked, "Is there any doubt what caused the bottle to fly across the room?" Recall in Chapter 5 I shared the story of how SET began when I was challenged to evaluate the cardiac care system. In that evaluation I observed that in one case the failure to appropriately secure the LUCAS2™ stabilization strap caused a patient's spleen to rupture, killing that patient. I did not wait, nor would it have been ethical to do so, for a sufficient number of observations to be sure that failing to use the stabilization strap was the cause of death. $N = 1$ observations was sufficient to draw a conclusion and make a recommendation.

Recommendation Timeliness

The traditional way evaluation findings and recommendations are conveyed to decision-makers is in a final report. As one of this book's reviewers adeptly noted "final reports are antithetical to a dynamic systems approach." From an evaluation use perspective, waiting to present decision-makers with a final report is problematic for a few reasons. First, final reports often contain numerous recommendations. It can be highly problematic for multiple recommendations to be simultaneously implemented. Systems and cultures need time to adjust and incremental change is preferred (Smith, 2020). Second, when simultaneously presented with multiple recommendations it can be difficult for decision-makers to know the best sequence in which to implement them. Further, it may be that some recommendations are themselves interdependent. Thus, a recommendation implemented earlier in a sequence may either alter subsequent recommendations or make them moot (J. Renger, personal communication, January 23, 2022). Third, the opportunity to implement some recommendations while "the iron is hot" is lost. Fourth, the assumption underlying a recommendation is that it is intended to make improvements. "Is it not then unethical to withhold recommendations that could bring benefit to the system actors and by extension to those the system serves because of an artificial construct like a final report?" Lastly, as Friedman notes, reports should be "simple, common sense, and accessible" (RBAclips, 2009, 2:11). A final report consisting of numerous recommendations is just the opposite and can create feelings of being overwhelmed. A typical reaction to such feelings is to shut down cognitively (Hurvich, 2000). Obviously, if the decision-maker shuts down, then the recommendations will not be used.

To meet the timeliness criterion, I recommend NRT evaluation as a viable alternative to the traditional, final report. NRT evaluation is defined as making findings and recommendations to the decision-maker as they are discovered during the course of the evaluation. Although NRT evolved in emergency management (Brusset et al., 2010), I have found system leaders welcome NRT recommendations (provided they are spaced appropriately; see "Sufficiently Frequent" criterion below) for presenting evaluation recommendations, because they act as micro-changes that do not overwhelm the system (Robin, 2014; Smith, 2020).

In practice, I meet with leaders and explain that I will be making recommendations as they become available. I negotiate how to convey NRT recommendations with the systems leaders and it usually takes the form of texts, emails, or a phone call. To operationalize NRT evaluations, I create a simple rule, asking that decision-makers respond to the recommendation within a week. They simply need to let me know whether they have decided to act on the recommendation. This simple agreement ensures the recommendations are considered and remain timely.

Sufficiently Frequent

This is one of the more challenging recommendation criteria to manage. The actual timing of detecting a system inefficiency may not be within the evaluator's control. The timing is further complicated by the fact that too many simultaneous recommendations can lead to the feelings of being overwhelmed; a form of system shock. On the other hand, waiting too long in-between recommendations can negatively impact the system leaders' and actors' motivation to participate in the evaluation.

In my experience, it is possible to manage the timing of recommendations. Often, especially at the beginning of the system evaluation, many inefficiencies are detected, each requiring a recommendation. As noted above, it isn't a good idea to present all the recommendations in a bundle; if you do that you essentially are replicating problems associated with the typical final report. The challenge then is knowing which recommendations to forward and when.

My simple rule is that any recommendation involving the safety or well-being of system actors or those the system is intended to serve must be addressed first.

I suggest starting with the recommendations that are easier and quicker to implement, such as completing additional training, making an IS change to fix a feedback loop, implementing a simple rule, and so forth. These micro-changes are usually easier to implement and can create small wins. Small wins "can increase momentum for change" (Foster-Fishman & Watson, 2011, p. 504).

Credibility

Credibility is built when recommendations meet two criteria: They must be congruent with the system leaders' and actors' lived experiences, and systems leaders and actors must experience success in implementing them. To meet the first criterion, you must ensure that the evaluation recommendations reflect the complexity, the reality, in which the intervention is operating. Following SET will ensure that the recommendations are aligned to this reality. To meet the second criterion, early recommendations should focus on incremental or micro-changes to help create small wins.

You can also help build credibility by managing expectations. Making changes to a complex intervention acting as a system can take time. Margaret Wheatley, noted that

> quick fixes are an oxymoron. If leaders would learn anything from the past many years, it's that there are no quick fixes. For most [systems], meaningful change is at least a three- to five-year process though this seems impossibly long. Yet multiyear change efforts are the hard reality we must face. (Barlow & Stone, 2011, p. 6)

Thus, you need to prepare system leaders for numerous evaluation recommendations being presented to them over time and, of course, follow-through on that expectation.

The Role of the Evaluation of the Emergent System Property in Deriving Recommendations

Thus far I've discussed how to make recommendations based on the evaluation of system efficiency (i.e., interdependencies). System efficiency recommendations can be made independent of an evaluation of system effectiveness (i.e., emergence). However, in my experience the reverse is not true. Making recommendations about system effectiveness cannot be done in isolation of system efficiency, because interdependence is a prerequisite for emergence. For example, assuming you have a valid measure of the essential system property and it fails to emerge, but the system parts are working together as they should, then you may need to re-engage leadership (or those served by the complex intervention) about whether the essential system property is correct (Chapter 9). Alternatively, if the essential system property does not emerge and the system parts are not working as they should, then recommendations should first focus on improving the system part interdependencies and/or revisiting whether all the system parts are correct. I developed the algorithm in Figure 10.1 to help you navigate how to synthesize the system efficiency and effectiveness evaluation findings to arrive at a recommendation.

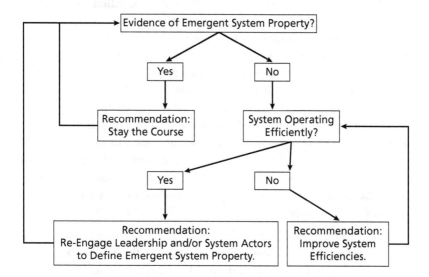

Figure 10.1 A decision algorithm for making system recommendations.

System Levels and Recommendations

As you learned in Chapter 3, systems can consist of many levels, layers, or subsystems. Dr. Lewe Atkinson from the Haines' Centre for Strategic Management taught me that sometimes the solution to a system problem can't be solved at the level you are operating; the solution may lie at the next highest system level.

Referring back to Mall of America example (Chapter 3), imagine that in the food court there were two establishments that catered to breakfast clientele and were struggling to keep the doors open, like a coffeehouse and a breakfast burrito restaurant. The food court needs these types of establishments to maintain the correct mix so that all types of customers who come to the food court leave happy. The evaluation of both establishments shows they are running efficiently and that the customers they serve are in fact leaving satisfied. Great coffee and yummy burritos. Applying the cascading failure systems principle, you learn that the problem is that both establishments aren't getting enough traffic because the mall does not open until 9:00 a.m. Thus, early rising customers don't see the mall as an option for their coffee and breakfast. If the mall opened earlier, say at 7:00 a.m., then this would increase customer traffic. Both establishments have the capacity of opening earlier, but the problem is the mall in which they are located, the system in which they reside, does not open its doors until 9:00 a.m. The solution resides at a higher system level in that the decision whether to open earlier must be made by the mall manager, who must weigh the entire system costs of opening earlier, such as increasing the hours of mall security.

Continuing to build on the Mall of America example, now imagine that the reason there is less customer traffic at the mall as a whole is because there isn't adequate parking. To solve this problem, the Mall of America manager and owner(s) need to annex more land for parking. This solution requires involving the next higher system level, the community and local government to rezone land for parking purposes.

Tracking Recommendations Use

One goal of making recommendations is to increase evaluation use. However, in my experience evaluators rarely, if ever, track whether our recommendations are used. In fact, I have been unable to find a single evaluation study reporting the degree to which evaluation recommendations are considered or adopted, nor their level of influence. I speculated on several reasons for this including the fear of facing the reality that our work isn't used at all (Renger, 2022).

I called for our field to begin collecting Evaluation Utility Metrics (EUMs; Renger, 2022). I suggested three types of EUM: The fraction of recommendations considered (EUM_c), adopted (EUM_a) and their level of influence (EUM_{li}).

$$EUM_C = \frac{\text{Evaluation Recommendations Considered}}{\text{Evaluation Recommendations Made}} \times 100$$

By negotiating the simple rule that leaders respond back to me within 1 week, I am able to routinely get 100% of my recommendations considered.

$$EUM_a = \frac{\text{Evaluation Recommendations Adopted}}{\text{Evaluation Recommendations Made}} \times 100$$

In my systems work the EUM_a ranges from 66%–85%. Naturally, there will be those factors beyond your control, like those found in any bureaucracy, that limit the likelihood of ever achieving 100% adoption. However, these adoption rates are significantly higher than those of any program evaluation I ever completed. It is my belief that this high utility rate is evidence that the recommendations derived from matching the evaluation approach to the problem and providing them in NRT lead to meaningful, actionable steps for system leaders and actors.

Assuming a recommendation is adopted then I suggest tracking its level of influence, or EUM_{li}. Measuring influence is less formulaic than measuring consideration or adoption, and requires the evaluator to engage in more extensive recommendation follow-up. A recommendation's level of influence ultimately depends on the number of system levels the client believes they can/should influence. For example, in my evaluation of a public health food safety division, leaders wanted to understand the extent to which adopted recommendations influenced their broader county health department and the county administrators. A recommendation that was able to make it to these higher levels, would have significantly more influence than if it stayed at the division level.

> While there is no actual data from which to compare, many of my colleagues have lamented how their evaluation reports are simply shelved; 0% utility. I suspect one reason evaluators don't collect data on the extent to which recommendations are considered, adopted, and/or their level of influence is because we "can't handle the truth."

Conclusion

The goal of any evaluation should be to have the information derived from the evaluation considered and used by those with the power to implement them. We cannot stop short and simply provide the findings of our evaluations, we must offer recommendations if our evaluations are to be useful. By following SET, you will be able to provide recommendations in NRT, which provides leaders and actors of complex interventions acting as systems an opportunity to make micro-changes. These micro-changes will result in small wins for you, the evaluator, building your credibility and increasing the likelihood of other recommendations being adopted.

While I've had success ensuring all my recommendations were considered, certainly not all of my recommendations were adopted. Sometimes, the reason they were not adopted was beyond my control, like politics. Sometimes, they were not adopted because a recommendation failed to consider an important contextual variable; in other words, I made a mistake. Remember, no matter how hard you try, the data will never be perfect and leaders understand that they "are privy to additional contextual information when weighing your recommendations and are always making decisions with imperfect data" (F. Garcia, chief medical officer, personal communication, May 30, 2021).

References

Barlow, Z., & Stone, M. K. (2011). Living systems and leadership: Cultivating conditions for institutional change. *Journal of Sustainability Education, 2*(1), 1–29.

Brusset, E., Cosgrave, J., & MacDonald, W. (2010). Real-time evaluation in humanitarian emergencies. *New Directions for Evaluation, 2010*(126), 9–20. https://doi.org/10.1002/ev.326

Burnes, B. (2005). Complexity theory and organizational change. *International Journal of Management Reviews, 7*(2), 73–90. https://doi.org/10.1111/j.1468-2370.2005.00107.x

Byrne, B. (2019, January 22). *Simple solution and complex problems—A lethal combination.* Kinch Lyons. https://kinchlyons.com/simple-solutions-and-complex-problems-a-lethal-combination/

Foster-Fishman, P., & Watson, E. (2011). The ABLe change framework: A conceptual and methodological tool for promoting systems change. *American Journal of Community Psychology, 49*(3–4), 503–516. https://doi.org/10.1007/s10464-011-9454-x

Friederici, P. (2009, March–April). *How a flock of birds can fly and move together.* Audubon. https://www.audubon.org/magazine/march-april-2009/how-flock-birds-can-fly-and-move-together

Gray, D. J. (1968). Value-free sociology: A doctrine of hypocrisy and irresponsibility. *The Sociological Quarterly, 9*(2), 176–185. https://www.jstor.org/stable/4105039

Henry, G. T. (2000). Why not use? *New Directions for Evaluation, 88,* 85–98. https://doi.org/10.1002/ev.1193

Henry, G. T. (2003). Influential evaluations. *American Journal of Evaluation, 24*(4), 515–524. https://doi.org/10.1177/109821400302400409

Henry, G. T., & Mark, M. (2003). Beyond use: Understanding evaluation's influence on attitudes and actions. *American Journal of Evaluation, 24*(3), 293–314. https://doi.org/10.1177/109821400302400302

Hurvich, M. (2000). Fear of being overwhelmed and psychoanalytic theories of anxiety. *Psychoanalytic Review, 87,* 615–650.

King, J. A., & Pechman, E. M. (1982). *The process of evaluation use in local school settings* (Final report of NIE Grant 81-0900). Orleans Parish School Board. https://files.eric.ed.gov/fulltext/ED233037.pdf

Mark, M. M., Henry, G. T., & Julnes, G. (2000). *Evaluation: An integrated framework for understanding, guiding, and improving policies and programs.* Jossey-Bass.

McCormick, E. R. (1997). *Factors influencing the use of evaluation results* [Unpublished Doctoral dissertation]. University of Minnesota.

Patton, M. Q. (2008). *Utilization-focused evaluation.* SAGE Publications. https://doi.org/10.1177/1098214010373646

RBAClips. (2009). *Video introduction to result based accountability by Mark Friedman* [Video]. YouTube. https://youtu.be/RtBC89F3Xi4

Renger, R., Renger, J., Van Eck, R. N., Basson, M. D., & Renger, J. (2022). Evaluation Utility Metrics (EUMs) in Reflective Practice. *Canadian Journal of Program Evaluation, 37*(1), 142–154.

Renger, R., Renger, J., Basson, M. D., Van Eck, R., Renger, J., Souvannasacd, E., & Hart, G. (2021). Using the Homeland Security and Exercise

Evaluation Program (HSEEP) building block approach to implement system evaluation theory (SET). *American Journal of Evaluation, 42*(4), 586–601 https://doi.org/10.1177/1098214020986619

Robin, V. (2014). *Blessing the hands that feeds us: Lessons from a 10-mile diet.* Penguin Books.

Scriven, M. (1991). *Evaluation thesaurus* (4th ed.). SAGE Publications.

Smith, C. (2020). *Pros and cons of incremental change vs the "big bang" approach.* The Change Management Blog. https://change.walkme.com/incremental-change/

Yarbrough, D. B. (2017). Developing the program utility standards: Scholarly foundations and collaborative processes. *Canadian Journal of Program Evaluation, 31*(3), 284–304. https://doi.org/10.3138/cjpe.349

Yarbrough, D. B., Shula, L. M., Hopson, R. K., & Caruthers, F. A. (2010). *The program evaluation standards: A guide for evaluators and evaluation users* (3rd. ed). Corwin Press.

11

Resistance to System Evaluation

The Dunning-Kruger perfect storm: Reductionists believe (incorrectly) that they are expert system evaluators and system evaluators assume (incorrectly) that reductionists are expert system evaluators.

By virtue of the fact that you are in the final chapter of this book it is likely safe to assume that you are open to using a systems evaluation approach in your practice or are already doing it. However, not all of our evaluation colleagues are as accepting of systems evaluation. I too was initially skeptical about systems approaches in evaluation because of my negative experience at the first annual systems evaluation conference (GIZ, 2011). I witnessed firsthand, session after session, the difficulty evaluators had speaking to each other about systems, systems thinking, and systems evaluation. Everyone had a different understanding and everyone had trouble practicing "intellectual humility" (M. Pescud, personal communication, March 3, 2020). I left the conference thinking that if we couldn't explain systems evaluation to ourselves (evaluators), then we shouldn't be rolling out the approach

System Evaluation Theory, pages 189–199
Copyright © 2022 by Information Age Publishing
www.infoagepub.com
189

to the public. I was concerned about the impact that a premature roll out might have on our discipline's credibility, that we would once again be accused of pushing what my trusted friend Laura Biesiadecki called the "evaluator flavor of the day" (Renger et al., 2011). So, I set out to create system evaluation theory (SET) in the hope of creating more coherence, confidence, and credibility within the field.

Since that GIZ conference I have been on my systems journey (Atkinson, 2020). With the help of friends and mentors like Drs. Mel Pescud and Lewe Atkinson, I came to better understand the barriers to applying systems thinking in evaluation. This chapter is devoted to sharing some of my observations as to the reason for this resistance. It is my hope that by understanding these resistances you can take the necessary countermeasures to prevent them from influencing your evaluation and perhaps sway others to embark on their journey so we can amass the critical mass of the brain trust necessary to keep advancing SET and methods.

The Perception That System Evaluators Are Elitists

Much of the systems evaluation literature is published by academics for academics. I myself was an academic for almost 30 years. During my tenure I was continually frustrated by what Dr. Barb Brown, a cherished mentor of mine who passed away far too early, called the conspicuous consumption phenomenon in academics. Conspicuous consumption is a sociological theory that, in layperson terms, says some people believe you need to look, act, and talk the part to be accepted into a group with which you desire to be affiliated. Corneo and Jeanne (1997) called it "snobbism" and my trusted friend Melanie calls it elitism (M. Pescud, personal communication, March 3, 2020).

In the academic world, snobbism translates to using unnecessarily sophisticated, exotic, (and often incorrect) language in an attempt to create the impression that you are a subject matter expert (Burnes, 2005). Comparing evaluation approaches, for example, on their ontological and epistemological differences or pontificating about the relationship between realist evaluation and emancipatory action are important to the academic evaluator but, as Oppenheimer (2006) found, using big words unnecessarily (and sometimes incorrectly) can create the opposite impression; namely, that you are pretender and not a contender.

Friedman said that we must do away with "jargon" when explaining evaluation (RBAClips, 2009, 2:36). Practitioners must find ways to explain systems evaluation approaches simply to those with whom they interact. To be perceived as an elitist will stifle cooperation, undermine trust, and be the death of a useful evaluation. As I said earlier in the book, we should be able to explain what we do, why we do it, and how we do to an 8-year-old in a 30-second elevator ride.

Throughout the book I did my best to use examples to explain, as simply as possible, how to define and evaluate complex interventions acting as systems. I encourage you to draw upon these examples or others from your experience to gain the buy-in you need from your clients and stakeholders to complete a useful evaluation; one that a decision-maker will use.

The Perception That Systems Evaluation Is Too Complicated

The most common argument I encounter from those resisting systems evaluation is that it is "too complicated." The word cloud in Figure 11.1 is from a workshop in which we asked evaluators what words they associated with systems.

The perception that systems evaluation is complicated isn't surprising when we, systems evaluation advocates, continually refer to complex interventions as "wicked," "super-wicked," or "messes" (Ison, 2010; Levin et al., 2012; Williams & van 't Hof, 2016). As Jonathan Morrell, the then editor of *Evaluation and Program Planning* once lamented: "Complexity is nothing more than non-linear relationships!" (J. Morrell, personal

Figure 11.1   Words evaluators associate with systems.

communication, February, 2018); a point echoed by another great, late systems thinker Barry Richmond (STELLA, 2003). We need to be cognizant of how terms that sound "cool" or "exotic" (Burnes, 2005) to us (i.e., systems evaluation advocates) may be creating barriers to evaluators wanting to pursue systems evaluation and clients wanting to work with us.

We must be aware of the first impression we make by the words we choose. It is not uncommon for systems evaluators to proudly display their causal loop diagrams (see Chapter 7). Using visual models *is* a recommended system practice for trying to convey complicated things simply (Australian Prevention Partnership Centre [APPC], 2018). As you know, I have used several visual aids throughout this book to convey SET and methods. However, sometimes the purpose of using an image to make things easier to understand is forgotten by academics. The literature is clear that when people are confronted with complexity, they often feel overwhelmed and this can cause them to seek relief by withdrawing (Kabigting, 2019; Watkins, 2012). In other words, using complex images may be deterring emerging evaluators from "embarking on their system thinking journey" all together because they convey the message that systems evaluation is complicated, or difficult (Atkinson, 2020). When people feel overwhelmed, they cope by reverting back to things that make them comfortable but are not necessarily the best option; like using program logic to evaluate a system.

If there is one thing that my over 25 years working in the medical sector taught me it is that you don't get a second chance to make a first impression (Ketikidis et al., 2012). If our first impression is that systems evaluation is too complicated and we lose someone's interest, then we have also lost the opportunity to add to the intellectual critical mass needed to keep advancing systems evaluation.

To be fair, I am certain the theory and work underpinning causal loop diagrams are of the highest standards. I also trust the results would make sense to those participating in its creation. My concern is that in our effort to impress we may overwhelm and/or foster resistance. So, I encourage you to use your discernment and adjust your use of diagrams and language according to your audience's needs.

The approach I recommend when giving a systems evaluation presentation is to follow what I term the "cooking show template." I always begin by explaining the ingredients I am using by defining systems thinking, systems, systems properties, and systems principles. I then show how each ingredient can be used by itself, like how the feedback loop principle can be added to improve our understanding of relationships. I then show how the ingredients can be combined, for example using the feedback loop and reflex arc principles to evaluate system efficiency. I end the presentation by showing the meal, the defined and evaluated complex intervention acting as a system. Since I took my audience along on the journey, they are less likely to see the complexity as complicated and less apt to be overwhelmed. Always walk alongside your clients rather than out in front.

> In my opinion it is the ineptitude, the need to feel self-important, and self-promotion of some evaluators that has unnecessarily complicated the evaluation of complex interventions.

The Clash Between Reductionist and Holistic Worldviews

Resistance to systems thinking can also stem from a difference between the reductionist and holistic worldviews (Systemic Thinking 101, 2018). As you learned throughout this book, when faced with a problem, those in the reductionist camp favor analysis, wanting to understand the problem by studying individual puzzle pieces. The belief is that understanding the basic building blocks is the key to understanding the universe because every effect has a cause. Ackoff uses the examples of physics drilling down to the most basic element, the atom, to explain the universe and biology drilling down to the most basic element, the cell, to explain life. The process of drilling down during analysis is called reductionism.

On the opposite end of the spectrum is the holistic worldview. In this worldview, to understand how something works you need to engage in synthesis, the opposite of analysis. Synthesis uses a bottom–up, rather than top–down approach. Ackoff illustrates synthesis by using a university example, but in reality all bureaucracies can serve as an example (Systemic Thinking 101, 2018). Ackoff explains that to understand why a university is structured and works the way it does you must understand the education system in which it is embedded (Systemic Thinking 101, 2018). For example, I taught in the Arizona higher education system for 17 years. To understand why Arizona State University (ASU) did not have a medical degree program you needed to understand that it is just one element (institution) of a larger higher education system. In this case the Arizona Board of Regents who coordinated higher education at the state level, decided the state could not support two medical schools and thus made a decision to offer that specialty through the University of Arizona. It would be difficult to understand why ASU did not have a medical degree program through analysis: breaking ASU down into its components, like colleges and departments, would never help understand why it did not have a medical program.

"What have the reductionist and holistic worldviews got to do with evaluation and resistance to system thinking?" Well, the evaluation discipline is heavily influenced by researchers whom I have referred to as the "wolves in sheep's clothing," reductionist trained colleagues who disguise themselves as evaluators (Renger, 2014). Michael Scriven (2013) gave a powerful talk at the Australian Evaluation Society Annual Conference where he warned that reductionist-trained researchers have "hijacked" our field, a sentiment shared by Dr. Michelle Irving (personal communication, June 26, 2021).

Researchers and evaluators typically have different objectives (although they sometimes overlap): the former to uncover new, generalizable knowledge, the latter to provide information to assist decision-making for interventions built on that research (Levin-Rozalis, 2003; Mark et al., 2000). In their search for knowledge, reductionist-trained researchers are taught to analyze, to reduce things to their basic elements, and to control the environment to establish cause and effect. Many reductionists argue that the randomized control trial is the only definitive way to establish cause and effect and should be the gold standard for evaluating programs (Bickman & Reich, 2014; Donaldson et al., 2015). The randomized control trial attempts to control all environmental factors to establish the definitive cause of any observed effect: It operates on the Ceteris Paribus principle, or all else equal. Just pause and think about that for a moment. "Does evaluating any intervention by trying to control all the other contextual factors make sense and reflect the real world?"

My experience resonates with Scriven's (2013) observations that many reductionist-trained researchers view evaluation and evaluators as inferior. They see the synthesis worldview as nonscientific. It reminds me of the view quantitative researchers had/have toward qualitative researchers, believing their methods are less credible and less valid. The truth is both worldviews are important and have their place. For example, consider the situation where the evaluation of our single fast-food restaurant (Chapter 3) found that repeat customers and revenues, our measures of the essential system property (i.e., a positive customer experience), were down. Using a reductionist approach, we could drill down to uncover why the problem might exist, for example by using methods like root cause analysis (Coşkun et al., 2012). Such an analysis might find customers were having a negative experience because of a poorly trained line staff person. Our recommendation might be to improve training or hire someone new. However, the answer to the problem may lie at the higher-level systems within which the fast-food restaurant is embedded; namely, the food court and the mall. For example, there may be less overall traffic to the food court because there are no restaurants in the food court subsystem offering vegan options or the shared seating space in the food court isn't being cleaned regularly. Or going up to the mall level, it could be that there is overall less traffic because an anchor store recently closed.

The point is that one approach to problem solving isn't better than the other, you may need to look up (synthesis) and/or drill down (analysis) to understand the issue and develop an appropriate recommendation. The goal is to use the right approach for the right evaluation purpose. So, cultivating discernment is key to becoming a good systems evaluator.

The Reality That Systems Evaluators Themselves Are Confused

I have attended numerous seminars and workshops on the topic of systems evaluation. It is my concern that those who come to these presentations with an open mind to learning leave confused and disinterested in pursuing their own systems evaluation journey. When systems evaluators communicate, they often appear to talk past each other. They fail to engage in the good system practice of listening deeply (APPC, 2018). As a result, there continues to be confusion between basic terminology such as systematic, systemic, and systems; and generally, what is meant by a systems evaluation (Bleich, 2014; GIZ, 2011).

Confusing terminology is common across many professions (DeJesus et al., 2019). Adding to the confusion is that systems thinking is used in so many disciplines each with its subtle variations in how they refer to and define the same principles (Ison, 2010). The result is that newcomers may perceive the systems arena as disjointed and disengage.

Barry Richmond noted the need for systems advocates to develop a common language and framework for sharing specialized knowledge (Arnold & Wade, 2015). Scriven (1991) also recognized this need when he published the evaluation thesaurus. Unfortunately, Scriven's work predated the rise of systems in evaluation. Thus, he only defines the terms system and systems approach tangentially as they relate to the concept of synthesis.

An example of how our careless use of terms can create problems is illustrated by the interchangeable use of the terms systems principles and systems concepts. The American Evaluation Association (2018) defines systems thinking as a "way of thinking based on core system concepts" (p. 6). By definition the term "concept" means the idea is still being formulated. However, many of these system concepts are in fact system *principles*, tested under a variety of conditions, in a variety of contexts, over an extended period of time. System principles are the proof of concept. Further, systems principles are robust, being successfully applied in computing, engineering, anthropology, conversation theory, mathematics, science, economics, sociology, terrorism, psychological well-being, natural resource management, and so on (Davis & Stroink, 2016; Ison, 2010; Monat & Gannon, 2015; Ossimitz, 1996). When we carelessly refer to principles as concepts it creates the impression that the science of systems is immature. In fact, the science of systems predates the discipline of evaluation. The impression that systems in its infancy can create barriers to others embracing systems evaluation.

Despite the best efforts of those like Scriven to establish a common nomenclature, we continue to talk past each other. When we find ourselves in one of these nebulous conversations, we often treat the situation like the tale of the emperor's new clothes. Instead of acknowledging there is an obvious disconnect and engaging in civil discourse, we choose to continue with a fruitless conversation. We must be willing to embrace discomfort and engage in the systems practices of questioning our assumptions (APPC, 2018), deep listening, and intellectual humility if we are to continually improve our efforts to evolve the field. Hopefully this book has armed you with the knowledge to recognize when there is a disconnect and to have the confidence to ask your colleagues for clarification about systems thinking, systems, and evaluating complex interventions operating and functioning as systems.

Conclusion

In this book you learned that often interventions acting as systems are complex, but the steps to defining and evaluating them need not be complicated. The work will sometimes be tedious, but with perseverance you will find yourself conducting and collaborating on more meaningful and rewarding evaluations.

The system's journey I took you on was methodical and deliberate. I endeavored to explain the why behind each step you learned because those who understand "the why?" are better able to explain complicated and complex theories and principles simply.

There is resistance to systems evaluation by fellow evaluators, and much of this, I believe, can be remedied by advocates of systems evaluation improving the way we communicate. Meaningful advancements in evaluation are made by double-loop and triple-loop learners, those who can elevate to another level of thinking (Argyris, 1976). They are focused on doing the right things and not just doing things right (Atkinson, 2020). Pioneers like Indigenous peoples, Donella Meadows, Peter Checkland, Derek Cabrera, Patricia Rogers, Melanie Pescud, Richard Hummelbrunner, Steve Haines, and Lewe Atkinson are double-loop learners who understood the limitations of analysis and reductionist approaches. They saw the potential of system thinking in other fields and introduced it as a solution to the limitations of program evaluation approaches. At times I have been critical of my colleagues, but recognize that it was their groundwork that helped advance my thinking. I hope this book honored their work and helped extend their thinking to the next level. I fully expect that I too will come under criticism, but that will be an indicator that our field is advancing, and that is the ultimate goal.

I am so enjoying my systems evaluation journey. The processes and products of my work have been so much more rewarding than those that emerged from my program evaluation work. I am hoping the table is now SET for you to move forward on your journey. I wish you luck and hope that one day, when the opportunity presents itself, you too will take the time to share your experiences and knowledge so that systems evaluation will continue to adapt and grow.

References

American Evaluation Association. (2018). *Principles for effective use of systems thinking in evaluation*. Systems in Evaluation TIG. https://www .aes.asn.au/images/stories/regions/QLD/SETIG-Principles-FINAL -DRAFT-2018-9-9.pdf

Argyris, C. (1976). Single-loop and double-loop models in research on decision-making. *Administrative Science Quarterly, 21*(3), 363–375. https://doi.org/10.2307/2391848

Arnold, R. D., & Wade, J. P. (2015). A definition of systems thinking: A systems approach. *Procedia computer science, 44*, 669–678. https://doi.org/10.1016/j.procs.2015.03.050

Atkinson, L. (2020, August). *AES Queensland Newsletter.*

Australian Prevention Partnership Centre. (2018). *Systems practices you can do every day.* https://preventioncentre.org.au/wp-content/uploads/2021/10/Systems-Thinking-A4-Poster_Aug18.pdf

Bickman, L., & Reich, S.M. (2015). Randomized control trials: A gold standard or gold plated? In S. I. Donaldson, C. A. Christie, & M. M. Mark (Eds.), *Credible and actionable evidence: The foundation for rigorous and influential evaluations* (2nd ed., pp. 83–114). SAGE.

Bleich, M. R. (2014). Developing leaders as system thinkers—Part I. *The Journal of Continuing Education in Nursing, 45*(4), 158–159. http://doi.org/10.3928/00220124-20140327-13

Burnes, B. (2005). Complexity theories and organizational change. *International Journal of Management Reviews, 7*(2), 73–90. https://doi.org/10.1111/j.1468-2370.2005.00107.x

Corneo, G., & Jeanne, O. (1997). Conspicuous consumption, snobbism, and conformism. *Journal of Public Economics, 66*(1), 55–71. https://doi.org/10.1016/S0047-2727(97)00016-9

Coşkun, R., Akande, A., & Renger, R. (2012). Using root cause analysis for evaluating program improvement. *Evaluation Journal of Australasia, 12*(2), 4–14. https://doi.org/10.1177/1035719X1201200202

Davis, A. C., & Stroink, M. L. (2016). The relationship between systems thinking and the new ecological paradigm. *Systems Research and Behavioral Science, 33*(4), 575–586. https://doi.org/10.1002/sres.2371

DeJesus, J. M., Callanan, M. A., Solis, G., & Gelman, S. A. (2019). Generic language in scientific communication. *Proceedings of the National Academy of Sciences of the United States of America, 116*(37), 18370–18377. https://doi.org/10.1073/pnas.1817706116

Donaldson, S. I., Christie, C. A., & Mark, M. M. (2015). *Credible and actionable evidence: The foundation for rigorous and influential evaluations* (2nd ed.). SAGE.

GIZ. (2011, January). *Conference proceedings.* Deutsche Gesellschaft fur International Zusammenarbeit (GIZ) Systemic Evaluation Conference, Eschborn, Germany. https://www.giz.de/en/html/about_giz.html

Ison, R. (2010). *Systems practice: How to act in a climate change world.* Springer. https://doi.org/10.1007/978-1-84996-125-7

Kabigting, E. N. R. (2019). Conceptual foreknowings: Integrative review of feeling overwhelmed. *Nursing Science Quarterly, 32*(1), 54–60. https://doi.org/10.1177/0894318418807931

Ketikidis, P., Dimitroviski, T., Lazuras, L., & Bath, P. A. (2012). Acceptance of health technology in health professionals: An application of the revised technology model. *Health Informatics Journal, 18*(2), 124–134. https://doi.org/10.1177/1460458211435425

Levin, K., Cashore, B., Bernstein, S., & Auld, G. (2012). Overcoming the tragedy of super wicked problems: Constraining our future selves to ameliorate global climate change. *Policy Sciences, 45*(2), 123–152. https://doi.org/10.1007/s11077-012-9151-0

Levin-Rozalis, M. (2003). Evaluation and research: Differences and similarities. *Canadian Journal of Program Evaluation, 18*(2), 1–31.

Mark, M. M., Henry, G. T., & Julnes, G. (2000). *Evaluation: An integrated framework for understanding, guiding, and improving policies and programs.* Jossey-Bass.

Monat, J. P., & Gannon, T. F. (2015). What is systems thinking? A review of selected literature plus recommendations. *American Journal of Systems Science, 4*(1), 11–26. https://doi.org/10.5923/j.ajss.20150401.02

Oppenheimer, D. M. (2006). Consequences of erudite vernacular utilized irrespective of necessity: Problems of using long word needlessly. *Applied Cognitive Psychology, 20*(2), 139–156. https://doi.org/10.1002/acp.1178

Ossimitz, G. (1996). *The development of systems thinking skills using systems dynamics modelling tools.* http://webdoc.sub.gwdg.de/ebook/e/gdm/1996/ossimitz.pdf

RBAClips. (2009, March 10). *Video introduction to result based accountability by Mark Friedman* [Video]. YouTube. https://youtu.be/RtBC89F3Xi4

Renger, R. (2014, June 15–18). *The wolf (researcher) in sheep's (evaluator's) clothing.* Canadian Evaluation Society Annual Conference, Ottawa, Canada.

Renger, R., Wood, S., Williamson, S., & Krapp, S. (2011). Systemic evaluation, impact evaluation, and logic models. *Evaluation Journal of Australasia, 11*(2), 24–30. https://doi.org/10.1177/1035719X1101100204

Scriven, M. (1991). *Evaluation thesaurus* (4th ed.). SAGE Publications.

Scriven, M. (2013, September 2–6). *Reconstructing the foundations of evaluation: Practical philosophy of science vs. positivist philosophy of science.* Plenary talk at the Australasian Evaluation Society Annual Conference, Brisbane, Australia.

STELLA. (2003). *An introduction to systems thinking.* High Performance Systems Inc. https://www.colorado.edu/center/mortenson/sites/default/files/attached-files/stella_ist_0.pdf

Systemic Thinking 101. (2018, February 5). *Russell L Ackoff from mechanistic to systemic thinking* [Video]. YouTube. https://www.youtube.com/watch?v=yGN5DBpW93g

Watkins, M. D. (2012). How managers become leaders. The seven seismic shifts of perspectives and responsibility. *The Harvard Business Review, 90*(6), 64–72. https://hbr.org/2012/06/how-managers-become-leaders

Williams, B., & van't Hof, S. (2016). *Wicked solutions: A systems approach to complex problems* (2nd ed.).

CPSIA information can be obtained
at www.ICGtesting.com
Printed in the USA
JSHW080853201122
33351JS00001B/20